KODIE BEDFORD was born in Geraldton, Western Australia, with strong family ties to East Kimberley. Her best memories consist of her listening to her family spin yarns recounting town legends, family feats and spilling the odd secret. It was solid training for storytelling and, after watching an episode of *Buffy the Vampire Slayer*, Kodie decided that she wanted to be a screenwriter.

Kodie moved to Sydney to work as a cadet journalist for SBS in 2008 for Indigenous current affairs program Living Black. She then worked at the ABC as a researcher/producer for documentary series Message Stick. Never forgetting her dream of wanting to be a screenwriter, Kodie made the jump to television drama where her credits include *Mystery Road* (ABC), *Summer Love* (ABC), *Firebite* (AMC+) and *All My Friends are Racist* (ABC). Kodie received the 2019 Balnaves Fellowship to develop her own play with Belvoir Theatre, *Cursed!*, which was staged in 2020 and won both best stage play and the major award at the 2021 Australian Writers' Guild Awards.

At home Kodie likes to drink copious amounts of tea, catch up on royal family news and spend time with rescue staffy Pocket.

Sacha Horler as Dawn Osborn in Belvoir's production of Cursed! *(Photo: Luke Currie-Richardson)*

Cursed!

Kodie Bedford

CURRENCY PRESS
The performing arts publisher

CURRENCY PLAYS

First published in 2022
by Currency Press Pty Ltd,
PO Box 2287, Strawberry Hills, NSW, 2012, Australia
enquiries@currency.com.au
www.currency.com.au

Typeset by Lucinda Naughton for Currency Press.
Cover design by Lisa White for Currency Press.

Currency Press acknowledges the Traditional Owners of the Country on which
we live and work. We pay our respects to all Aboriginal and Torres Strait
Islander Elders, past and present.

A catalogue record for this
book is available from the
National Library of Australia

NATIONAL
LIBRARY
OF AUSTRALIA

Contents

Introduction   vii

CURSED!

   Act One   1

   Act Two   48

Introduction

'The only people for me are the mad ones, the ones who are mad to live, mad to talk, mad to be saved, desirous of everything at the same time, the ones who never yawn or say a commonplace thing, but burn, burn, burn like the fabulous yellow roman candles exploding like spiders across the sky.'

Jack Kerouac, *On the Road*

Comedy is the hardest frame from which to view trauma because it requires the darkest dramatic tensions to be wrangled into the light. Kodie Bedford's *Cursed!* is a microscopic slice of Australian history blown up and examined with unashamed truth and rigour. The play takes our fears of who we are in relation to our families and in doing so exposes our fears of who we are as a nation.

We have begun a new age of understanding the 'mind'. It seems to have taken a long time for Eastern philosophies, temporarily popular with the baby boomers, to permeate the zeitgeist of capitalism. Perhaps this is a result of the existential conundrum the individual faces when choosing to embrace the pharmacology of mental wellness. Until recently, discussion and treatment around mental illness was kept a close secret by individuals and families seeking social 'normality'.

I have never read a more irreverently funny first draft than the one Kodie Bedford sent me at the beginning of making this work. Apart from being outrageously 'naughty' (reminiscent of the English playwright Joe Orton), I was struck by how honest the play is about inherited mental illness. The terrifying curse of waking up to the fact that your family has passed on genetic and behavioural issues is a common anecdote as we come into an age where people can speak more openly about such things. And nothing has more potential to make mental illness bloom like a catalytic flower than grief. The confrontation of mortality can do strange things to the most stable of families, but here, the Osborns have been obtusely avoiding what can be described as another level of 'madness', bringing us, the audience, into a heightened world of tragicomic proportions.

Set in the sleepy town of Geraldton, Western Australia, the wind blows sand everywhere, pervading everything and no matter how much our matriarch Dawn vacuums, the particles of the long history of the Yamaji people, the Dutch and the *Batavia*, the English colonisers or the multigenerational immigrants arriving by sea, the sedimentary remnants of our nation's past will never be separated from who Dawn is or who we are. Dawn's 'bipolarness' is writ large here, equally entertaining and terrifying the audience as she copes with the loss of a parent and the reuniting of a family so genetically disparate that the audience may question if it could be real. It is real and we know it is because the burning truth of Bedford's voice sits behind all these wonderfully crafted, recognisable characters that always surprise and never fail to remind us of the reality that we are a mongrel nation. With our mongrel nature comes an honest crassness that defies modern 'outrage culture' because it is, after all, true.

The complexities of our national character exist in regional places. Often regional people and places are treated with contempt or complacency in contemporary artistic thought because they do not fit comfortably into our political or social progression and remind a lot of city dwellers of where they have come from and perhaps what they are running from. Racism is a generationally transmitted disease. It is not only an immediate familial predicament, but a historic national predicament that refuses to die out. Just as the Osborns keep secrets from each other, our contemporary social discourse is the result of historical secrets buried in the myth-making of our Australian identity. Casual racism and 'seemingly tolerant' prejudice have been a cornerstone of the Australian family and its relationship to society. Nowhere is this more on display than in regional townships. The metropolitan centres of our country have learnt to hide it and generationally we have different responses to such intolerant derision and different methods for coping with such transgressions.

Ritual plays an enormous role in family gatherings. What happens if your familial culture is so diverse that 'authentic' ritual no longer seems important or is now intangible? The Osborns, like other Australian families, must devise their own. Here, Bedford delves into the absurd rules and structures families impose on themselves to glue themselves to each other. Games of role within the family change and surprise, giving the audience delightful hilarity while reminding us that deep melancholy is also a game that has to be played raw and honest. There are brutal truths, either delivered like skipping stones on a firm surface of comic broadness or as incisively deep cuts of despair. It creates a beautifully affirming experience for the audience. As Australians, we are all complicit in the national game of identity through comedy.

We, as a nation, have often defined ourselves in relation to the 'other' but at the same time we have just as often claimed that we are 'fair'. This oppositional complexity of being both tolerant and intolerant is masterfully comic. This sly weapon of truth is on powerful show in Kodie Bedford's wonderful play and just like the hereditary nature of mental health, this problematic complexity is passed down through families. Unless we can accept the curse of who we are, only then can we have hope of ever breaking it.

Jason Klarwein
Jason Klarwein is a freelance actor/director and the current Artistic Director of the Grin and Tonic Theatre Troupe.

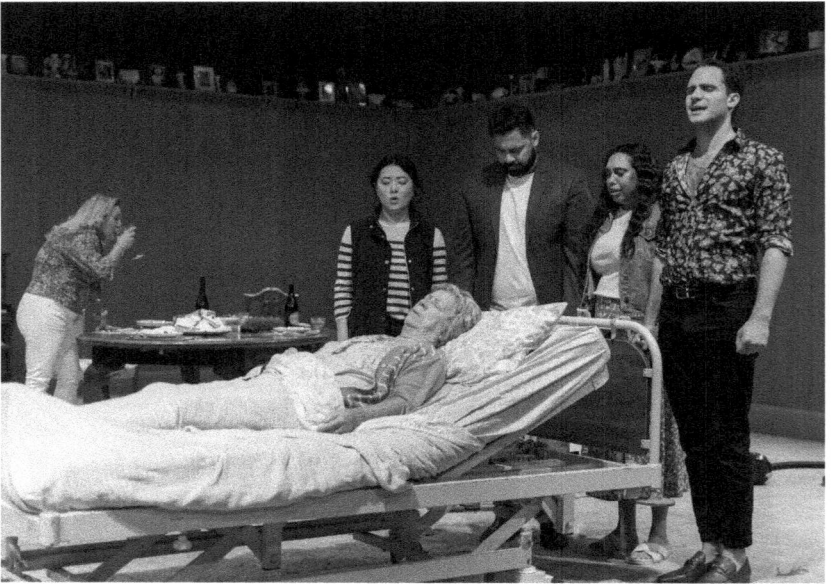

Sacha Horler, Shirong Wu, Valerie Bader, Bjorn Stewart, Chenoa Deemal and Alex Stylianou in Belvoir's production of Cursed! *(Photo by Luke Currie-Richardson)*

Cursed! was first produced by Belvoir at Belvoir St Theatre, Sydney, on 24 October 2022, with the following cast:

VAL OSBORN (NAN) / MILDRED TRUNFULL	Valerie Bader
DAWN OSBORN	Sacha Horler
SEBASTIAN OSBORN	Alex Stylianou
MARIE OSBORN	Shirong Wu
BERNADETTE OSBORN	Chenoa Deemal
IZZY WATTS	Bjorn Stewart

Director, Jason Klarwein
Set Designer, Stephen Curtis
Costume Designer, Chloe Greaves
Lighting Designer, Chloe Ogilvie
Composer and Sound Designer, Steve Francis
Assistant Director, Dalara Williams
Assistant Costume Designer, Keerthi Subramanyam
Associate Lighting Designer, Veronique Benett
Movement/Fight Director, Nigel Poulton
Stage Manager, Natalie Moir
Assistant Stage Manager, Brooke Verburg

Indigenous theatre at Belvoir supported by The Balnaves Foundation.

CHARACTERS

VAL OSBORN (NAN), 70 years old, grandmother. English heritage.

DAWN OSBORN, 50 years old, Val's daughter. English heritage.

SEBASTIAN OSBORN, 32 years old, eldest child, son of Dawn. Maltese heritage.

MARIE OSBORN, 30 years old, daughter of Dawn. Chinese heritage.

BERNADETTE OSBORN, 28 years old, youngest child, daughter of Dawn. Aboriginal.

IZZY WATTS, 30 years old, Charlie's boyfriend. Aboriginal.

MILDRED TRUNFULL, 65 years old, Val's sister. English heritage.

SETTING

Geraldton, Western Australia. 400 kilometres north of Perth. The Midwest of Australia.

Specifically set in a blue fibro house, although it doesn't have to be blue, it's just my memory. It's public housing built in the 1960s— it doesn't protect you from heat or cold which can be a problem in the searing summer, but luckily it has wooden windows to let in the afternoon sea breeze. The front room sits directly opposite the lighthouse, which continually cycles the spinning light. It can drive a person mad.

There is also a scene on a psychiatrist's couch.

NOTES

Doubling suggestions:

Val / Mildred

People this play will offend: Blackfellas, whitefellas, Catholics (and anyone who believes in Jesus), LGBTIQ+, vegans, blind Portuguese people, Vietnamese grudge holders, alcoholics, bogans, Gerotonians, people with Alzheimer's, horny great aunts, people with mental illness.

The writer has love for those listed.

ACT ONE

SCENE ONE—A DREAM OF CALM SEAS

'Delta Dawn' starts playing.

BERNADETTE OSBORN *is dressed in a bright floral dress, a flower is in her hair, maybe she's even wearing a flowered lanyard. She has obviously just come from a party, a really cool Sydney house party—maybe in the inner west. But she isn't acting like she's just come from a party. She looks fucking miserable and a little dishevelled ... okay a lot dishevelled. She looks like she had a hard night of rosé and then passed out with her make-up still intact.*

A psychiatrist office.

BERNADETTE OSBORN *lies on a clichéd therapy couch awkwardly trying to get through a session. She can take off her flowers and wipe off her make-up, making herself look 'normal' during this speech.*

BERNADETTE: I've never been to therapy before. I know what you'll say. Blame my childhood. Isn't that what they say? That's the prime time for fast-tracking fuck-ups. But I can tell you right now it wasn't my childhood ... I mean, sure, my earliest memories are visiting my mother in a mental institution but I can say with confidence that my childhood was completely normal ... Apart from the mental institution bit. There are many adult reasons why a person can be depressed. Mortgage stress for example. I don't have a mortgage but if I had one, particularly here in Sydney, I would be very depressed. And I don't have any prospects of buying a house because both of my parents live in public housing and I have no equity to borrow off. It's a relief really. So I guess my point is that I'm not depressed about mortgages and I really don't know why I had a breakdown at Louisa's Hawaiian themed thirtieth birthday party in Surry Hills. It just came upon me. We could be talking about anything; all the pressures of modern day life. Climate change. Politics. Catholics. I'm not Catholic but I was raised as a Catholic and went to Catholic school. I wasn't molested or anything. Sorry, when you say to people you went to a

Catholic school, you immediately have to assure them you weren't touched. And if you were, that's a conversation stopper. Not that there's anything wrong with that. I mean there *is* something wrong with that. Shit. I'm sorry. Is that what I need to talk about in these sessions? Catholics? The non-touched variety of Catholics. Nan who raised us was as devout as they came. I'm talking rosary every night with my brother and sister. Praying for people—alcoholics, heathens, racists, Great Aunt Mildred who ticks all three boxes. But come to think of it, I don't think being a Catholic made me depressed. And it wasn't my childhood. Nan gave us a loving, sane, safe, somewhat Catholic (non-touched) childhood! Good country living. Geraldton in the Midwest of Western Australian. Yeah no-one has heard of it. But it is famous for the Batavia massacre, rape and pillaging. [*Smiling*] I miss it. [*Realising*] Not the massacre or rape or pillaging. I just miss the place. It may be a little more conservative but it's simple. People over here in the east complicate shit. Even racism is complicated—you have 'institutional racism', 'lateral violence', 'micro aggression'… sometimes I just miss the WA simplicity of being called a black cunt. Simplicity is good for me.

BERNADETTE *listens to the psychiatrist.*

It's not a cultural issue? Oh no no no … My black family are good, solid … middle class. No, no … this is my white side. They're still trying to find their place in the world.

Bernadette's phone rings.

Mum I'll call you back.

She hangs up.

Sorry about that. She's probably in a bit of a state.

Bernadette's phone rings again. She rejects the call.

It's all under control.

Oh, we don't need to talk about my mother.

Bernadette's phone rings again and she answers it.

Jesus fucking Christ I'm in the middle of something! [*Listening*] Oh fuck.

SCENE TWO—VOYAGE

Suddenly we're at Nan's fibro house. It may be a little rough and weather worn around the edges but you can tell it's been loved and cared for with little touches that only a grandmother can give it; vinca flowers in the garden, Geraldton wax too, seashells and an array of lighthouse garden features. Never mind the real lighthouse that's opposite the house—red and white candy stripes and 34 metres high. The lamp at the top of the lighthouse cycles through the day and night as a warning to ships and possibly BERNADETTE.

BERNADETTE *arrives at the house dragging her suitcase and pillow (bringing your pillow is a very WA thing to do). She carries a box of Krispy Kremes as well.*

She looks up at the lighthouse.

There are sounds of the waves and wind. It's almost peaceful.

She's home. She breathes in the air. She closes her eyes. She smiles.

Then:

A vacuum turns on.

BERNADETTE *frowns. Oh right … she's home.*

Maybe she'll come back later.

She turns around to head out but is confronted by MARIE OSBORN.

BERNADETTE: Marie, you scared me.
MARIE: Sorry. I just saw you.
BERNADETTE: Have you been sitting in your car?
MARIE: Yes.
BERNADETTE: For how long?
MARIE: Three hours.
BERNADETTE: Three hours? You haven't gone in for three hours?

> *The vacuuming grows more aggressive.*

Good call.

> *Marie's phone rings.*

MARIE: [*into the phone*] Hello? Yeah it's in the crisper. Yeah I'm here. Bernadette just got here. [*To* BERNADETTE] Matt says hi. [*To phone*]

Yep. I'll Skype them tonight for a bedtime story at six forty-five pm. Have them bathed by six thirty pm. Use the coconut oil. No, organic. Right. Call me in fifteen. Bye.

BERNADETTE: You didn't bring the kids?

MARIE: They don't need to see this. I don't need to see this. It's a very inconvenient time. I'm supposed to be organising cupcakes for the daycare this week. I put a lot of parents out. I just know they're talking about me in that little group chat of theirs. They don't buy the excuse family emergency anymore. That's how ruthless they are.

> MARIE *starts digging in her bag for her flask. She finds it and takes a swig.*

BERNADETTE: So it's true? She's not funnin' this time?

MARIE: I don't know. Mum's in a state and you can never count on the truth when she's in a state … So you go in and see.

> BERNADETTE *stands there. Willing herself to go in. Can she? Can she? No she can't.*

BERNADETTE: Wait, has Sebastian arrived?

MARIE: I haven't heard from him.

BERNADETTE: He sent me a text yesterday saying he was boarding a plane in Portugal.

> BERNADETTE *looks at her phone, calculating the travel time in her head.*

MARIE: Glad to see he texts *you.*

BERNADETTE: He should be here … soon then?

MARIE: Soon.

BERNADETTE: Soon.

> *They stand there—not wanting to go in. The vacuum revs up.*

MARIE: Maybe we should wait for him in the car.

> *Yes they will. They go to walk away when* DAWN *bursts through the front door with her vacuum, ready to empty the bag into the garden. She sees* BERNADETTE *and* MARIE.

DAWN: Aghhhhh!

> DAWN *rushes forward to give them a hug.* BERNADETTE *accepts it.* MARIE *is more cold, her arms remain at her sides.*

My darling girls. When did you get here?

BERNADETTE *and* MARIE: [*together*] Just now.

DAWN *pinches* BERNADETTE*'s cheeks like she's a baby. She grabs for the Krispy Kremes.*

DAWN: I wish you called, I could have got tea ready, I could have got my hair done … Oh are these those flash city donuts I saw on *Dr. Phil?* Some woman was addicted to them. All she ate. Shaped like a donut too. Can't wait to try them. The flashiest afternoon tea ever. Looks like you've been sneaking some.

DAWN *pokes* BERNADETTE *in the stomach.*

BERNADETTE: Thanks, I'm well.

DAWN: Don't be a Sensitive Sally.

BERNADETTE: Is Sebastian here?

DAWN: He's in Singapore. If you want duty free perfume text him now. I'm going cha-neel. Georgio from the hairdresser is going Lou-ess Vytonne. Marg from the canteen has gone one of them Kardashians. Marie you ought to change up your style a little bit, looking a bit mummy-frump. Georgio, Marg and I are gonna be the slickest smelling gals chucking mainies down town. Maybe get you a new daddy.

MARIE *and* BERNADETTE *are quite uncomfortable.*

MARIE: Another one.

BERNADETTE *interjects before an argument breaks out.*

BERNADETTE: Okay. Mum … fashion and weight aside, you called us here for Nan.

DAWN: She's been a bloody bore. Dying is an extremely boring process, I tell you. [*Off* BERNADETTE *and* MARIE*'s reactions*] Well, see for yourself. Excuse the mess, bloody wind blowing its guts out.

DAWN *goes inside as* MARIE *pulls* BERNADETTE *aside.*

MARIE: Don't let her come between us.

MARIE *goes inside.* BERNADETTE *takes one last look to the lighthouse. One last look to sanity.*

SCENE THREE—BLESSING OF THE FLEET

The interior of the house looks like it was decorated in the 1960s and little has changed. There are lighthouse ornaments and a scattering of family photos—the kind you're embarrassed to see in adulthood.

There's a piano in the living room that hasn't been played in years. The dining chairs are on top of the dining table (so DAWN *can easily vacuum).*

And in the centre, NAN *lies in a hospital-like bed on wheels, close to death.* BERNADETTE *follows* DAWN *and* MARIE *into the living room.*

They stop and see NAN. *It's a bit of a shock.*

No-one knows what to say. They haven't seen their nan like this. She's vulnerable. She's helpless. She's—

DAWN: Do you want lunch? Ham was on special this week. I can make some sandwiches.

> BERNADETTE *kneels by* NAN *and delicately takes her hand.* MARIE *deliberately stays by the door.*

BERNADETTE: How long has she been like this?

DAWN: [*shrugging*] A week?

MARIE: So she's not funnin'?

DAWN: It would be impressive funnin' if she was. She hasn't even got the rattles yet so she's got some time. She's probably waiting for Sebastian. He was her favourite.

MARIE: Nan has no favourites.

DAWN: She does. Sebastian.

MARIE: That's your favourite.

DAWN: Oh yeah. Probably waiting for Bernadette then. She was her favourite.

MARIE: Nice.

BERNADETTE: You should have called us earlier.

DAWN: I thought she was funnin' those first few days. Then the doctor came and said get your affairs in order so I booked into Georgio's …

BERNADETTE: You went to the hairdresser?

MARIE: What the hell?

DAWN: Well if you two are going to gang up on me, you can turn right around and go to your flash lives. This place is like a bloody zoo, is it

so wrong to want to look good? I've been doing all the work looking
after Nan here while you two and your brother are off gallivanting.
MARIE: I live on a farm three hundred kilometres away, and I'm raising
twins. If anyone is gallivanting, it's Bernadette.
BERNADETTE: I am not gallivanting! I call in every day from Sydney. I
even answer calls during daylight savings.
DAWN: I don't believe in daylight savings. Fades the curtains.
MARIE: Okay. I'll just drop changing nappies and the bedtime routine
and warming their formula—
DAWN: Just feed them with ya tits.
MARIE: I can't. And before you say anything, it's actually quite normal
for babies to have problems latching onto their mother's breasts.
It's a process.
DAWN: Maybe if you weren't off gallivanting, Marie.
MARIE: I'm out.

MARIE *goes to leave.*

BERNADETTE: Marie. Don't leave. We're here for Nan.

MARIE *reluctantly agrees.*

DAWN: I stand by gallivanting.
BERNADETTE: Stand by it all you want. I hired you a nurse to help out.
MARIE: And I chucked in money for that nurse …

MARIE *looks around, realising.*

Where is the nurse?
DAWN: [*avoiding eye contact*] I'll go make some ham sandwiches. You
must be tired.
BERNADETTE: Stop! … Where's the nurse?

DAWN *doubles down.*

DAWN: I told her to go home.
MARIE: Why?
DAWN: No use both of us waiting for Jesus to come get her.
MARIE: You let her go?
DAWN: What's a few days? That nurse deserves it. Nan is hard work.
Treated her like …

DAWN *looks around like someone is watching.*

[*Whispering*] A slave.

> DAWN *starts spray and wiping the dining table.*

BERNADETTE: Why are you whispering?

DAWN: She was African. The last words out of Nan's mouth was calling her a traitor. I was trying to watch *Home and Away* and Nan is carrying on about how this poor woman was trying to poison her. Lucky I'm good with the blacks, hey Bernadette. Her people have been through a lot, you know.

BERNADETTE: People? She was born and raised in Perth. Her name is Sharon. I read her CV.

DAWN: Perth people have been through a lot too. There's a drought on. Don't be a racist.

MARIE: Oh God. We paid the nurse to look after Nan from twelve pm to eight pm because you were complaining non-stop about missing *Home and Away*.

DAWN: I still missed the finale. How else will I know if McKenzie got married or died in a house fire?

MARIE: Bernadette, tell Mum we need that nurse back.

DAWN: Bernadette, tell your sister we can manage.

> BERNADETTE *looks at* MARIE *and* DAWN. *She's torn but she's a problem solver.*

BERNADETTE: Okay. Look, we're here now so we can look after Nan.

DAWN: Ha!

MARIE: I knew you'd take her side.

DAWN: Because I'm right.

BERNADETTE: I'm not taking sides.

MARIE: Another waste of money.

DAWN: Who needs money? Can't take it with you.

MARIE: Okay for someone who's never had to work for it. Still on Centrelink, Mum? Taxpayer money funding your carefree lifestyle. New clothes, Dawn?

DAWN: I may live with the commoners, Marie, but I'm still a fashion plate. You ought to take my fashion advice from time to time.

MARIE: Oh yay, mutton dressed as lamb.

DAWN: Or in your case mutton dressed as mutton.

BERNADETTE: HEY! Let's just concentrate on Nan. That's what we're here for. Mum go make some ham sandwiches.

DAWN: I'll even make it fancy. Parsley on top, paid by the taxpayer.

DAWN exits.

MARIE: She's off her meds.

BERNADETTE: She's stressed.

MARIE: I don't appreciate my breastfeeding being made fun of.

BERNADETTE: No-one is making fun of it Marie, just ignore her and she won't take continuous bites.

MARIE: Here we go again. The chaos. The jibes. The yelling. The threats. The tears. All of that (s-h-i-t) that comes with this endless drama. This time, I've got a family to look after and zero time for cyclone Dawn.

BERNADETTE: I'll take care of things.

Marie's phone rings.

I have a plan.

MARIE looks BERNADETTE up and down.

MARIE: Fine. [*Into the phone*] Matt. No, they have to take a nap or they'll be grumpy. I scheduled it for forty-five minutes.

BERNADETTE is left with NAN alone. She takes her hand.

BERNADETTE: I have a plan. You wake up.

BERNADETTE fixes up NAN's hair.

BERNADETTE gets up and goes over to the piano. She sits down and plays a key.

SCENE FOUR—MEMORIES OF CALM WATERS

NAN sits up hearing the key. BERNADETTE becomes eight years old.

NAN: No thumpedies!

YOUNG BERNADETTE: But I have to play loud. It says forte and you won't let me use the pedals.

NAN: You can use the pedals when you stop your thumpedies.

YOUNG BERNADETTE: I don't want to play anymore. Can't we go outside and play?

NAN: You haven't done your scales.

YOUNG BERNADETTE: The sun is out.

NAN: And the southerly will come in any moment and blow it all to the whoops. God gave you a talent to make your nanny happy. You don't know when she'll die.

YOUNG BERNADETTE: Are you poorly?

NAN: God could take me any minute. Now you better play me something nice. 'Fur Elise' maybe.

YOUNG BERNADETTE: I hate that song.

NAN: Classical blasphemy.

YOUNG BERNADETTE: Nan? Why do you always say you're going to die?

NAN: Because it's true. One day I'm going to heaven and so we have to make the most of having Nanny here. Like playing the piano when she asks.

YOUNG BERNADETTE: I don't want to play the piano anymore.

NAN: What next? Drugs? You tempt a path to hell and God wants all of his children in heaven.

YOUNG BERNADETTE: Do you think the Batavia murderers are in heaven?

NAN: Depends how many people they killed. What was it? Five, six?

YOUNG BERNADETTE: One hundred and ten men, women and children were massacred.

NAN: Well in that case, they're probably in hell with Hitler and rock musicians.

YOUNG BERNADETTE: Is Mum going to hell? I heard you on the phone last night.

NAN: Little pigs have big ears. Don't worry about her, she's just in a state.

YOUNG BERNADETTE: Is she coming to my Batavia talk? I've practiced really hard.

NAN: I doubt the doctors will let her. But we'll pray.

YOUNG BERNADETTE: Will you come to my Batavia talk, Nan?

NAN: Of course. Now no more questions. If you're not going to play me 'Fur Elise', do your scales. Scales are a good foundation to music. You can never be too prepared.

SCENE FIVE—ROUGH SEAS AHEAD

Back to the present. DAWN *bursts into the lounge room with ten ham sandwiches with parsley piled on top of them.*

DAWN: You can never be too prepared.

BERNADETTE: How many people are you feeding?

DAWN *looks down at* BERNADETTE*'s stomach.*

DAWN: Well, someone looks like they have a healthy appetite, that's all. Where's sour tits?

BERNADETTE: She's sensitive about the breastfeeding Mum, so stop.

DAWN: What's there to be sensitive about? We're family, no judgement! Even when she was a teenager she was like that about her boobs.

BERNADETTE: Because you told her she couldn't pull off a bikini at surf club. You said she had pirates' disease.

DAWN *and* BERNADETTE: [*together*] Sunken chest. Ha!

BERNADETTE: Didn't really give her confidence.

DAWN: So it's my fault she's dried up?

BERNADETTE: Mum, listen to me. That nurse was meant to help out.

DAWN: Not this again.

BERNADETTE: Are you … in a state?

DAWN: Excuse me but my mother's dying. It's all very stressful. Do you know how much affairs there are to order in death? There's so much to do in so little hours. Casseroles being dropped off every night. The priest comes over and I got to get the fine china out because God forbid he drinks out of common Kmart-ware. Then I got to go get Nan's lotto, put her numbers in—because she'd know if I didn't get it and haunt my white arse for the rest of my days. But on the way to lotto I run into bloody Candy who's got to know the ins and outs of a duck's arse, discussing the price of canola. I come home, Harry from two doors down calls. He's not the brightest tool in the paddock and so have to help find his keys. And I still got a list as long as a donkey's dick. I've got to go into Georgio's hair salon for a wash and blow-dry, must look slickered, and prep Marg from the canteen who wants to do catering for the funeral. Plus book the Maoris to sing in the service. He's a bit of a spunk that one, always gotta show my nice side.

DAWN *pushes her bra up.*

Then I gotta see unfortunate Gary for a cuppa. He looks great since he got off the ice. And then I gotta clean the house, love it's all just go, go, go.

BERNADETTE: So you're in a state.

DAWN: I get more stuff done if I'm … in a state.

BERNADETTE: That's not a reason.

DAWN: It is! How else am I meant to keep this family together? Marie's got tittie and personality problems. And Sebastian has his own worries—it's hard being a world class opera singer. And you …

BERNADETTE: What about me?

DAWN: You seem different.

Beat.

MARIE *walks back in.*

MARIE: What the hell is that outside?

DAWN: Oh you saw it?

BERNADETTE: What's outside?

DAWN: My caravan.

MARIE: A caravan.

BERNADETTE: A caravan?

DAWN: It was only five hundred bucks on buy and sell.

MARIE: You don't have five hundred bucks.

DAWN: I saved for it.

MARIE: That's why she got rid of the nurse. She kept the money.

DAWN: I obey the Lord's commandments. Well maybe that one time from the school canteen but that was a misunderstanding. I had fifty dollars left on my pension and I put it on a quaddie, okay?

MARIE: Did you hear that Bernadette? She's gambling.

BERNADETTE: I'm standing right here.

DAWN: Bernadette, I don't judge your eastern state lifestyle choices.

BERNADETTE: You were meant to stick to that budget I gave you.

DAWN: I earned that caravan fair and square. It's my dream. It's always been my dream. I'm gonna fix her up, I'm gonna paint her up and drive off across the Nullarbor.

MARIE *and* BERNADETTE *look at each other confused.*

BERNADETTE: What the hell is across the Nullarbor?

DAWN: Freedom. Adventure. Adelaide.

MARIE: Don't be ridiculous.

DAWN: As soon as [*nodding over to* NAN] buggalugs leaves … I'll be in the dust.

MARIE: That van is going. Bernadette?

BERNADETTE *thinks. She looks at* DAWN *who is pleading with her eyes.*

DAWN: Bernadette?

BERNADETTE: You can't drive across the Nullarbor.

DAWN: You're nothing but a pair of moles. And you're not selling my dream!

DAWN *runs out.* MARIE *chases after her.*

MARIE: Don't even think about chaining yourself to the van!

BERNADETTE *is left alone. She looks at her phone. She goes to dial. But she can't. She looks at* NAN. *She grabs a paper out of the draw and dials a number. She walks out as:*

SCENE SIX—PIRATES AND TREASURE

Hooray! For SEBASTIAN *has finally arrived.*

SEBASTIAN *walks in, arm in arm with* DAWN *(who's carrying a plate of Krispy Kremes and a new handbag).* MARIE *follows them carrying Sebastian's suitcase. They sit down at the table.* SEBASTIAN *is very animated as he recounts his European trip and* DAWN *is just as enthralled.* MARIE *isn't as polite. She's bored.*

SEBASTIAN: It was like a real moment of enlightenment. And fate. They said, 'Sebastian, you've got to go on. There is no other person who can do this'. And so I went out. Single spotlight. I couldn't see out to the audience, but I could feel their eyes on me, waiting for me. I nodded to the conductor and he raised his baton. It was now or never. I took a deep breath and sung out. My diaphragm aching, my vocal chords shaking and I forgot where I was. I could've been back in the cathedral singing for Christmas mass. But I was in Paris. And the lead tenor had got hit by a car so I had to step in. I finished my solo and there was a moment of silence. Oh no they hate it. And then—

SEBASTIAN *starts clapping.*

DAWN *gives a round of applause.* MARIE *feigns a smile.*

A round of applause. Oh hi Nan.

It was honestly the most *magnifique* night of my life.

DAWN: My son … the French opera star. Isn't he fancy?

MARIE: The fanciest. What show was this?

SEBASTIAN: *Pirates of Penzance.*

DAWN: A classic.

DAWN *hugs her bag.*

I just love this handbag.

SEBASTIAN: Real leather too. And the stitching is from alpaca hair sewn by blind Portuguese women who live down the road from me. It's a real traditional technique.

DAWN: I love a traditional technique.

SEBASTIAN *hands out more presents.*

SEBASTIAN: Oh perfume for Mother, and here's the perfume for Georgio and Marg. And the bottle of whiskey for Robbo. Isn't Robbo an alcoholic?

DAWN: Alcoholics are the easiest to buy presents for when you want something done. He's gonna help me fix up my caravan.

SEBASTIAN: What caravan?

MARIE: Apparently she has a Nullarbor dream.

DAWN: Adelaide!

BERNADETTE *comes in holding her phone.*

BERNADETTE: Do you know where Nan kept her other bills? I'm trying to get through to the gas company and they need the customer number.

DAWN: No. I have not an inkling.

SEBASTIAN *pulls out another present from his bag.*

SEBASTIAN: And for my darling sisters.

MARIE *holds up an eye mask and* BERNADETTE *holds up a neck pillow—obvious airport gifts.*

MARIE *and* BERNADETTE: [*together*] You shouldn't have.

BERNADETTE *starts searching through the drawers for the gas bill.*

SEBASTIAN: Oh and a scarf for Nan.

DAWN: She should wear that in her coffin. It would be the first thing you'd look at. Draw your eye away from her corpse.

SEBASTIAN: This was sewn by poor southern French prostitutes now living as nuns in the mountains.

SEBASTIAN *walks over and dresses* NAN *in his scarf.*

DAWN: Oh way too good for her coffin. I think I better take that.

MARIE: Have we finished the European stories?

DAWN: Oh I hope not. I could listen to them forever and ever.

SEBASTIAN: You know the Portuguese have this saying '*Ir com os porcos.*'

DAWN: [*repeating* SEBASTIAN] '*Ir com os porcos.*'

SEBASTIAN: It means to go with the pigs. To die.

DAWN: I like the Portuguese way of thinking. It's a bit sexy.

BERNADETTE: [*on the phone*] Yes I'm here. No I haven't found it yet. I can't put Valda on. She's in a fucking coma.

> BERNADETTE *hangs up frustratedly. She continues searching for the bill.* DAWN *discretely shifts the bills from a drawer to down her top during the following dialogue.*

MARIE: So you're not living in London anymore?

SEBASTIAN: London is so 2012. And full of Aussies. If I wanted to hang with bogans I would've stayed here, bought a Holden and hung in the Maccas car park at late night shopping. Or moved in with you.

MARIE: Hello, I married rich. I'm classy now.

BERNADETTE: Why Portugal?

SEBASTIAN: Portugal is way cheaper and only a two-hour train ride away. I do most of the opera training in the afternoon.

> MARIE *is suspicious.*

DAWN: I thought you had a Portuguese girl up your sleeve.

SEBASTIAN: I was seeing this woman named Esmerelda but she had an ex-husband who was … like a mafia boss or something. I don't do complication.

DAWN: Oh you don't want to date a divorcee.

MARIE: Says the woman who's been married three times.

DAWN: I'm the exception to the rule, Marie.

BERNADETTE: Remember how Nan always wanted Sebastian to marry Mary-Ann. She still held hopes that you would, you know.

SEBASTIAN: Oh yeah.

DAWN: Who's Mary-Ann?

MARIE: Mary-Ann.

SEBASTIAN: The one I took to the year ten spring dance.

DAWN: I don't remember that.

MARIE: You probably weren't here.

BERNADETTE: You know Mary-Ann—she was in the choir.

DAWN thinks. She can't picture her.

SEBASTIAN: The blonde one.

BERNADETTE: With scrunchy on top.

MARIE: She always did the first reading at Mass.

Still no recognition.

SEBASTIAN: She had a slight cock mouth when she sang.

He re-enacts the slight cock mouth.

DAWN: Oh Mary-Ann the mouth! She's lovely. You should definitely marry her. Make sure she gets rid of the cock-mouth … [*Nudging* SEBASTIAN] Or not!

SEBASTIAN: I'm friends with her on Facebook. She's married to a farmer.

DAWN: A farmer's wife like you Marie.

MARIE: I'm *not* a farmer's wife.

SEBASTIAN: Aren't you married to a farmer?

MARIE: Yes but I'm not defined as a farmer's wife.

SEBASTIAN: Moderator of the local Mums and Bubs Facebook page doesn't count.

MARIE: It actually involves a lot of work, Sebastian. You wouldn't know about that. I'm carrying a torch for working women.

DAWN: You one of those fancy feminists now, Marie? Just need a good cock and a razor.

BERNADETTE: Nothing wrong with being a feminist.

MARIE: Next she'll tell us not to vote.

DAWN: Haven't voted since 1996. Don't believe in it. Like daylight savings.

MARIE: That's terrible. It's your democratic right.

SEBASTIAN: Who knew Marie was such a democratic freedom fighter?

DAWN: Didn't know you had lots of time on the farm for such shit!

MARIE: I'll have you know I handed out pamphlets last election. That's how much I believe in this democracy.

BERNADETTE: Who for?

MARIE: What?

BERNADETTE: Who did you hand pamphlets out for?

MARIE: Oh just a local who was on the ticket.

BERNADETTE: Who?

MARIE: I don't want to get into it, Bernadette.

SEBASTIAN: Why? Did they lose?

MARIE: No, they won.

BERNADETTE: John Trudgett … the racist senator?

DAWN: Who does he hate? The blacks, the terrorists, or the Asians?

SEBASTIAN: All of the above.

BERNADETTE: Shame on you, Marie.

MARIE: Not everything is race related. John Trudgett does a lot for the farming communities. Without him, a lot of farmers who are the salt of this earth would be suffering in silence. Not everyone lives in the city and has university degrees, Bernadette.

BERNADETTE: It doesn't take a university degree to work out the things John Trudgett has said are completely offensive and his supporters are racist.

MARIE: I'm not racist. I'm bi-racial.

DAWN: What's bi-racial?

SEBASTIAN: It means, Mummy, that you had a lot of coloured cock.

DAWN: It's not the colour of it. It's how you use it.

BERNADETTE *spies something in Dawn's shirt. She grabs at it and pulls out the paper.*

BERNADETTE: The gas bill with the customer number.

DAWN: Oh there it is.

BERNADETTE: What else are you hiding?

DAWN: Oh Bernadette. I have it all under control.

BERNADETTE: Well now it's under my control.

DAWN *is annoyed.*

DAWN: You know what we all need? A good cup of tea. You can heal the world with a cup of tea. That's what Nan used to say. How do you want it? White like me, black like Bernadette, sweet like Sebastian or sour like …

MARIE: Do we still have to do that?

DAWN: You're the one voting for a racist when you're Chinese, your sister is black, your brother is a wog.

DAWN *leaves for the kitchen.*

No-one wants to talk.

MARIE: I wish Nan was awake. She'd put her back in the box.

SEBASTIAN: She seems fine to me.

MARIE: Sebastian living a life oblivious to it all. It must be nice.

BERNADETTE: I suppose we should talk about plans.

SEBASTIAN: She's going to wake up. Jesus owes her one.

BERNADETTE: But in the case that she doesn't recover … We have to decide where Mum is going.

Beat.

MARIE *and* SEBASTIAN: [*together*] I vote Bernadette.

BERNADETTE: Me?

MARIE: That's why I love a democracy.

SEBASTIAN: I live in Portugal. She doesn't even have a passport.

MARIE: I've got two kids and a farm.

SEBASTIAN: Plus Marie's running a very busy Facebook page, fighting for feminists, farmers and racists.

MARIE: Out of all of us, Bernadette, you have the special talent for keeping her … level. Mum came to my house for a week after the twins were born and left after day two. She always calls you first when she has a problem.

SEBASTIAN: You're the new family glue.

MARIE: It's what Nan would want.

BERNADETTE: And if I can't? Or won't?

DAWN *comes to the door holding a tray of tea and pumpkin scones—overhearing everything.*

MARIE: Could commit her.

SEBASTIAN: Again.

DAWN *walks in. Feigning not being upset. She hands out tea and towelettes with the scones.*

DAWN: Bernadette—plates. Push the old duck back for dinner. What do youse want for tea? I've got Carol from number ten's apricot chicken, Georgio's tuna mornay or Sandra the egg lady's shepherd's pie? I can't testify to her cooking but I can testify to her eggs.

BERNADETTE: I'm not hungry.

MARIE: I'm not hungry either.

SEBASTIAN: I ate on the plane. And I'm going out.

MARIE: I'm going to go out too.

BERNADETTE: You're both leaving?

SEBASTIAN: I've got to get out for a while.

MARIE: I've got to call into Cecilia's.

SEBASTIAN: [*teasing*] Oh Cecilia with the flat forehead.

MARIE: She can't help it.

BERNADETTE: You're not leaving.

> DAWN *throws down a glass and it smashes. Everyone goes silent.*

DAWN: APRICOT CHICKEN, TUNA MORNAY OR SHEPHERD'S PIE?

BERNADETTE, MARIE *and* SEBASTIAN: [*together*] Apricot chicken.

DAWN: I'll defrost the tuna mornay.

> DAWN *grabs the vacuum cleaner.* SEBASTIAN *and* MARIE *push* BERNADETTE *forward.*

BERNADETTE: Mum.

> BERNADETTE*'s words are drowned out by* DAWN *vacuuming vigorously. The floor. The table. The ceiling. The floor again.*
>
> *The kids sit on the couch, observing the vacuuming.*

Mum!

DAWN: I'm fine and dandy, darling. Just preparing the place. You can never be too prepared. Especially when my kids want to commit me.

SEBASTIAN: Marie said it, not me.

BERNADETTE: Mum, we don't want to commit you. We want to bring about an open dialogue regarding a future without Nan. Call it contingency planning.

DAWN: Those are big fancy words. Where did you learn that?

> DAWN *vacuums more aggressively.*

BERNADETTE: Mum, we care about you.

DAWN: I'm not going back to the nuthouse.

BERNADETTE: No, you're not. I wouldn't let that happen. You're healthy and looking the best I've seen you. You're sexy as.

> DAWN *stops vacuuming. She takes pride in her appearance.*

DAWN: I have been doing Jennifer Aniston's divorcee diet.

SEBASTIAN: It shows.

DAWN: I could even give Marie some tips.

MARIE: Great.

BERNADETTE: There see. We're all staying for dinner. As a family. As Nan would want it …

> BERNADETTE *glares at* MARIE *and* SEBASTIAN.

SEBASTIAN: Fine.

MARIE: Yes.

DAWN: Look at this mess.

> DAWN *starts vacuuming under* NAN *but she knocks Nan's bed.*

> *Something starts beeping.*

BERNADETTE: Turn it off!

DAWN: Oh fuck I've killed her!

MARIE: Is she dead?

> SEBASTIAN *makes the sign of the cross.*

SEBASTIAN: Please no.

> *Everyone is shocked. The beeping continues.*

DAWN: Someone check.

> MARIE *pushes* BERNADETTE *forward.* BERNADETTE *kneels and listens to* NAN*'s heart. Something isn't right. She follows the IV drip and picks up … A morphine case.*

BERNADETTE: It's just the morphine pump. She's still alive!

> SEBASTIAN *makes the sign of the cross again. Everyone is relieved.* DAWN *claps.*

DAWN: Christ! That was close, ay.

> DAWN *laughs.*

> MARIE *helps* BERNADETTE *put the morphine IV drip back in.*

SEBASTIAN: Come on Mum. Let's get a drink. Where's the nurse?

DAWN, MARIE *and* BERNADETTE: [*together*] Don't ask!

> DAWN, MARIE *and* SEBASTIAN *leave in different directions.*

> BERNADETTE *turns to* NAN.

SCENE SEVEN—EXPLORING PAST VOYAGES

Flashback, BERNADETTE *rings* NAN. NAN *picks up.*

NAN: Are you safe?

BERNADETTE: Yes I'm safe.

NAN: Are there murderers in Sydney?

BERNADETTE: They haven't murdered me yet.

NAN: Have you got the rosary beads I sent you?

BERNADETTE: Yes and the two job ads.

NAN: Just in case you decide to come home. Be a big fish in a little pond.

BERNADETTE: Nan something happened to me. I was swimming at La Perouse. I go there because it looks like the sun sets over the ocean, like in WA. I don't like the beaches here. Too crowded and rocky. But I went under the water and I suddenly panicked. I couldn't breathe. I felt like something bad was going to happen. I kept thinking of the Batavia. The murders and the mutiny. The survivors and the dread they felt. Being isolated on the edge of the earth, thinking this is it. I haven't thought of that since my talk in primary school.

> NAN *is silent.*

NAN: I'm sorry I wasn't there.

BERNADETTE: No Nan, I didn't mean to bring up that day.

NAN: I blame myself.

BERNADETTE: Forget it, let's talk about something else. How's Mum?

NAN: She's just got a bout of melancholy, she'll get over it.

BERNADETTE: Where is she?

NAN: She's in her room. I take in sandwiches and she yells all the obscenities under the sun at me. It would even make a sailor blush. But I suppose I'm to blame for that as well.

BERNADETTE: You're not to blame, Nan. You're perfect.

NAN: I'm poorly.

BERNADETTE: Do you want me to come home?

NAN: Yes, I do, but I need someone to see the world for me. Swim in the big ponds while you can. Home will always be here. Swim my little fish.

> NAN *lies back down.*

BERNADETTE *sits in the present. The southerly comes in.*

SEBASTIAN *walks in.*

SEBASTIAN: You call?

BERNADETTE: Reminiscing. Spend some time with her, while you can.

BERNADETTE *leaves* SEBASTIAN *with* NAN. SEBASTIAN *takes a seat next to* NAN. *It's uncomfortable. He pulls out his phone. He takes a selfie with her.*

SEBASTIAN *stops, waits, nothing. He puts his phone away.*

SEBASTIAN: You just wanted to get us back here right? I'm here. Back from being a Parisian opera star like you always wanted. You said I made you really proud and I like making you proud. I've been meaning to call … but I just needed to go out and discover … myself … the world. There's so many wonderful places that you'd love Nanny. Europe is basically Catholic Disneyland.

Beat.

God? It's my fault, isn't it? You won't bring her back because of me. Here's the deal, Nan comes back, I'll be holy for the rest of my life. A saint even. I'll marry Mary-Ann. There. You have it. Everything Nan wanted in me. One time offer. Living the life as a saint.

Sebastian's phone buzzes. He looks at it.

Barring the next ten minutes. Stay put.

SEBASTIAN *goes outside.*

SCENE EIGHT—STEERING OFF COURSE

SEBASTIAN *scrolls through his phone making sure no-one is watching him.* IZZY *arrives at the gate.* SEBASTIAN *looks down at his phone—he looks up.*

SEBASTIAN: You don't look like your picture.

IZZY: Pardon?

SEBASTIAN *shrugs.*

SEBASTIAN: Oh well. We'll have to go around the side.

SEBASTIAN *undoes his zip and goes in for a kiss.*

IZZY: Whoa!

SEBASTIAN: BottomSlutForU?

IZZY: Bottom slut?

SEBASTIAN: For you?

IZZY: For me?

SEBASTIAN: For me?

IZZY: For who?

SEBASTIAN: Not you?

IZZY: Not me.

SEBASTIAN: Not a bottom?

IZZY: Or a slut … For … you. I'm here for Bernadette.

SEBASTIAN: Oh shit.

> SEBASTIAN *quickly does up his zipper.*

BERNADETTE: Sebastian?

> BERNADETTE *comes out.*

Izzy?

IZZY: Oh good, you're okay.

> IZZY *turns around and starts to walk away.*

BERNADETTE: Wait. I just tried to call you. You came here?

IZZY: Had to check if you were alive. You kind of left without any note. You've been ignoring my phone calls and texts. The only way I could think of getting an answer was flying here which, by the way, is more expensive than flying to London.

BERNADETTE: We can talk but not here …

> But it's too late for BERNADETTE; MARIE *and* DAWN *join them outside.*

DAWN: … and then Mackenzie bursts into flames. What's going on? Who's this big handsome gentleman?

SEBASTIAN: Not someone I, I mean Bernadette, was expecting, obviously.

IZZY: Don't worry, I'm leaving.

BERNADETTE: Wait. It was an emergency, Izzy. My grandmother is on her deathbed.

IZZY: Why didn't you tell me? I'm your fiancé!

MARIE *and* SEBASTIAN: [*together*] Fiancé?!

Everyone looks at DAWN *for her reaction.*

DAWN: Would you like a ham sandwich and a cup of tea?

IZZY: Excuse me?

DAWN: Son-in-law!

BERNADETTE: Mum, go inside.

DAWN: Why? I'm very accommodating. Especially to blackfellas, unlike Marie.

MARIE: What?

BERNADETTE: Take her inside.

SEBASTIAN: Okay Mummy, time to let them talk.

SEBASTIAN *pushes* DAWN *in.*

MARIE: By the way, I *am* accommodating to blackfellas. Welcome.

MARIE *awkwardly bows.*

BERNADETTE: Please stop.

MARIE: I'll be inside.

MARIE *goes inside leaving* BERNADETTE *and* IZZY *alone. They stand in silence.*

Beat.

IZZY *and* BERNADETTE: [*together*] Listen.

IZZY: You go.

BERNADETTE: I'll try and get you on a flight first thing tomorrow.

IZZY: That's it? No apology? No 'Sorry Izzy'? You owe me an explanation.

BERNADETTE: I'm a little busy dealing with my grandmother.

IZZY: Is she really dying?

BERNADETTE: Yes. And on top of that I've broken up a fight between my mother and sister and my sister and brother, and me and my mother, and me and my sister. I'm trying to organise living arrangements and death arrangements of a stray family on the edge because I was voted in charge for a job I'm not qualified for. Now what is it you want to talk about?

IZZY *reaches into his jacket and pulls out some folded pieces of paper. He unfolds them. They're his notes. He flicks through, trying to find the words. He goes back to the beginning. He clears his throat ready to read.*

IZZY: Dear Bernadette …

> *He looks at* BERNADETTE. *He can't say it. He puts down his notes.* IZZY *submits. He puts the papers back in his pocket.*

I'm sorry. You never said anything about your family situation.

BERNADETTE: For good reason.

IZZY: Is there a good reason?

BERNADETTE: Many but none I can give you.

> *Beat.*

IZZY: Okay. But I have another problem.

BERNADETTE: What?

IZZY: I don't have money for a hotel. I maxed out my only credit card on this flight.

> BERNADETTE *is uncomfortable with the idea but concedes.*

BERNADETTE: Okay. But if you're going to stay here the night I have rules.

IZZY: Yes?

BERNADETTE: Don't be left in a room with my mother alone, don't ask my sister about who she voted for, you can ask my brother questions but don't get him started on his European stories and if my mother asks you if you want to hear her sing, say no.

IZZY: Is that all?

BERNADETTE: They're different to me. Just brace yourself.

IZZY: It can't be that bad.

> *They walk inside.*

SCENE NINE—YO HO HO AND A BOTTLE OF RUM

SEBASTIAN *and* MARIE *set the table.* MARIE *moves the donuts to the end of the table.*

MARIE: She's ashamed of us. Can you believe?

SEBASTIAN: There's a reason why I don't bring a partner over.

MARIE: [*laughing*] Partner?

SEBASTIAN: What?

MARIE: All this Mary-Ann talk and her c-o-c-k mouth? Is that a problem if she's a woman?

SEBASTIAN: What?

MARIE: I remember. Hamilton Smith.

SEBASTIAN: Whatever. Stop being a mole.

MARIE: Hamilton Smith asked me out on the foreshore.

SEBASTIAN: Oh here we go.

MARIE: I'd been dreaming of the day for years. I told you that I wanted him to take me to the high school ball. On ball night, I was running a little late, hair style problems with my newly cut bangs and I asked you to take Hamilton for a walk and entertain him as I fix my bang emergency. When you hadn't returned I went to go look. Imagine my surprise when I find my brother on his knees behind the lighthouse cottage with Hamilton. All these questions of why? Maybe my brother doesn't show loyalty. Maybe my brother is like his own father who cheated on our mother. Maybe my brother—

SEBASTIAN: Gives better head?

MARIE: I knew it.

SEBASTIAN: You know nothing. I was just helping the guy with his pants.

MARIE: Such a liar.

SEBASTIAN: And you're a bitch with bad bangs.

MARIE: Shame on you Sebastian.

SEBASTIAN: That was over ten years ago. But let me guess … you haven't left high school. All of your friends are from high school, and you talk about high school things, bring up your high school friends' kids together and then send your kids to the same high school. You're just jealous Bernadette and I left town and you got married to a farmer who is, let me guess, from our high school. Hashtag sad and delusional.

MARIE: Delusional? You're the one lying. I'm an integral part of farmer's wives' community. Who are you? A big … [*whispering*] p-o-o-f.

SEBASTIAN: Poof! Take that back!

MARIE: You take the hashtag sad and delusional back!

> *They start slapping each other.*

> DAWN *strides in with a baked tuna mornay … And they quickly stop.* DAWN *doesn't take notice.*

DAWN: Blowing its guts out.

SEBASTIAN: Tuna Mornay. Mmm …

> DAWN *cuts up the tuna mornay. She gets a bottle of passion pop.*

MARIE: I don't think Bernadette will like that.

DAWN: Nonsense. We are celebrating an engagement. Even got the fancy wine for the city folk.

MARIE: Passion pop?

SEBASTIAN: I think it's an ex-engagement.

DAWN: Not if I have anything to do with it.

MARIE: I wouldn't be playing Gero matchmaker.

DAWN: It's what I'm good at. I set up unfortunate Gary with Cindy Gobmother.

MARIE: I don't dare ask.

DAWN: She gives the best gobbies in Gero.

SEBASTIAN *and* DAWN: [*together*] Lucky him.

> DAWN *takes a swig of the passion pop and raises her glass.*

DAWN: To the gobmother.

MARIE: I'm not toasting to vulgar talk.

DAWN: Marie, you forget where you come from.

MARIE: I know I come from Geraldton.

DAWN: I meant my hole.

> DAWN *and* SEBASTIAN *laugh loudly.* BERNADETTE *strides in.*

BERNADETTE: No questions.

SEBASTIAN: About what? Your secret fiancé turning up on our doorstep?

BERNADETTE: No questions. That's rule number one. Rule number two, no drinking.

> BERNADETTE *snatches the passion pop off* DAWN.

DAWN: I don't subscribe to rules, Bernadette.

BERNADETTE: Well that changes today. I'll even make the rule specific. No asking personal questions, no asking about our relationship, no asking about reconciliation.

DAWN: Racist—

BERNADETTE: No saying you're not racist because you've had coloured cock like you told Marie's first boyfriend, Hamilton.

DAWN: I said that?

MARIE: Unfortunately yes.

SEBASTIAN: I'm told Hamilton could relate.

> MARIE *glares at* SEBASTIAN.

DAWN: What can we talk about then?

BERNADETTE: The weather. That's it. No further questions beyond that.

> *They hear footsteps. Everyone is tense as* IZZY *walks in.* IZZY *takes a seat.*

IZZY: Hello. Nice to meet you.

DAWN: So Izzy, tell us your life story?

BERNADETTE: What did I just say?

DAWN: To talk about the weather. Wind blows its guts out constantly. Gives us the whoops. Conversation over.

BERNADETTE: Let's just eat.

DAWN: We have tuna mornay. It's a simple country recipe. Or if you prefer city food, Bernadette brought Krispy Kremes.

IZZY: Tuna sounds great.

DAWN: Pass Izzy some mornay.

> SEBASTIAN *does.*

IZZY: This looks amazing Mrs Osborn.

DAWN: Oh I'm no Mrs anymore. All three of my husbands divorced me—

MARIE: How's the weather in Sydney?

IZZY: A bit rainy. Humid.

SEBASTIAN: Humid! Wow! You know in Europe—

MARIE: Can we stop with Europe.

DAWN: Izzy … That has a lot of z's. Just gives your tongue a nice little buzz when you say it. Izz-zee.

BERNADETTE: Jesus, Mum.

DAWN: Mind the blasphemy. Izzy, my daughter seems to think you're not interested in a proper conversation.

IZZY: Oh I don't mind.

DAWN: See.

IZZY: [*to* BERNADETTE] It's fine. It's your family. And it's a fabulous dinner.

BERNADETTE: Go for it then.

DAWN: So you're Aboriginal. I mean, I'm obviously a whitey but I know a little Yamatji.

SEBASTIAN: Oh God. She's gonna start talking in language.

DAWN: Ay jurdu means 'hey sis', Jackie down at the post office calls me that. 'Hey Jurdu, you white dawg!' She's so funny. That's our little joke. What's your word for sister?

IZZY: Umm … 'sis.'

DAWN: Lovely. Bernadette never teaches me language.

BERNADETTE: I don't know any language.

DAWN: That's a shame. Why not?

BERNADETTE: Because invasion and colonisation forced Indigenous peoples to assimilate or die. It's called cultural genocide.

DAWN: They're big fancy words. Where'd you learn them?

BERNADETTE: University.

MARIE: This is worst dinner conversation ever.

DAWN: My Marie votes for John Trudgett—the town racist. But he has good policies for farmers.

BERNADETTE: [*standing up*] I need to speak to you in private.

DAWN: There's no secrets in this family. To hell with your rules.

SEBASTIAN: It's true. Don't even think about wanking in the room.

DAWN: Sebastian I was cool about your wanking. I even washed your cock sock. And folded it.

SEBASTIAN: Thank you for letting everyone know.

MARIE: I will pay someone to talk about the weather.

DAWN: The point is we keep an open household. I'm cruizzy, like your name Izzy.

> DAWN *pulls out another bottle of passion pop from under the table, tears off the lid with her teeth and takes a swig. Marie's phone starts ringing.*

MARIE: Thank God. [*Answering*] Hi Matt.

> MARIE *walks out.*

DAWN: Don't mention her titties either. She's a bit sensitive about it.

> BERNADETTE *stands up.*

BERNADETTE: Kitchen. Now.

DAWN: Uh-oh. Mummy is in trouble.

> BERNADETTE *pushes* DAWN *into the kitchen.*

SEBASTIAN: I'm really sorry.

IZZY: It's a stressful time for your family.

SEBASTIAN: Oh not about her. Actually I'm talking about out there.

IZZY: Oh. [*Realising*] Oh! Don't worry about it.

SEBASTIAN: I don't normally …

IZZY: You don't have to explain.

SEBASTIAN: I'm not …

IZZY: Bottom Slut for You. It's okay. I'm from Sydney. I probably know more about gay sex than … I don't know anyone in the closet though.

SEBASTIAN: Well more … one foot in here and one foot and every other body part out there. I was raised a Catholic.

IZZY: Have you thought about telling?

SEBASTIAN: God no. Not on my Nan's dying breath. She prayed hard for me to get into heaven. Certainly not about to ruin that with knowledge of trying to hook up a bottom slut.

IZZY: For you.

SEBASTIAN: Mum would be dramatic … whenever we told her bad news she would make us act out her funeral, usually to Mariah, Celine or Whitney. No wonder I'm gay. It would only happen every now and then. Like after she broke up with Bernadette's dad. God that was 'My Heart Will Go On'. She'd put me in charge of the CD player, Marie was on flowers and Bernadette would say the eulogy. But I can't go through a fake funeral right now. I like to keep everyone happy, not cause any ripples that will lead to an inquisition on me.

> SEBASTIAN *pulls out some pills from his pocket and takes two.*

I've upped my anxiety pills. You want one?

IZZY: I'm not a psychologist, but I think you'd feel better just telling … at least telling your Nan. You wouldn't have to live with the lie.

SEBASTIAN: The lie is easier. It's what Xanax is for.

> BERNADETTE *and* DAWN *walk in and* SEBASTIAN *shoves the pills back into his pocket.* DAWN *holds a teacup.*

BERNADETTE: Hey hey … [*To* DAWN] Be calm. Be … cool.

DAWN: Cool as a cucumber. The green kind.

BERNADETTE: Where's Marie?

SEBASTIAN: On the phone.

BERNADETTE: I'll go get her.

> As soon as BERNADETTE *leaves the room* DAWN *fills her tea cup with passion pop.*

DAWN: It's like living with the fun police. Was it like that with you Izzy? Sebastian get some more booze.

SEBASTIAN *pulls out a passion pop bottle from behind the piano.*

IZZY: Oh nah. It was good.

DAWN: So you were living with her?

IZZY: Only for this year.

DAWN: I just don't understand why Bernadette tried to hide you from us, Izzy.

IZZY: I'm sorry. She never talked about you guys.

DAWN: And here you are … apologising for my daughter. Interesting. Typical her. Treat 'em mean, keep 'em keen. That's her mantra.

SEBASTIAN: [*to* DAWN] I thought that was yours.

DAWN: So does she?

IZZY: What?

DAWN: Get you to apologise first? Nothing is ever her fault?

IZZY: Well it's sometimes my fault. I'm really indecisive. She hates that. Sometimes. Maybe not all the time. Or maybe it was all the time. I don't know. I had this note I wrote on the plane, took me five hours. I'm not great at writing. I tend to overthink it. But I really wanted to read it to her because it said how I felt when she left. I looked up and she had it on her face like she wasn't even prepared to listen to my side even though she's the one who left without a trace.

DAWN *takes a devious sip.*

DAWN: You can read it to me, darling. If it means that much to you.

IZZY *prepares to read. He clears his throat …*

IZZY: Well now I feel guilty.

He looks over to NAN.

I haven't even met …

DAWN: Go introduce yourself. She's not racist …

IZZY *cautiously walks over.*

IZZY: Hi I'm Izzy. Nice to meet you. Sorry I didn't meet you sooner.

IZZY *grabs* NAN*'s hand. Shakes it. It falls down heavily.*

Sorry.

IZZY *tries to gently put* NAN's *arm back into place.*

DAWN: Don't be sorry. Catholics are all about forgiveness.

SEBASTIAN: They are?

DAWN: Unless you're divorced or gay. You're free to touch up someone though.

IZZY: I don't know what to do.

DAWN: Darling, Izzy. All good soul searching starts with a drink.

DAWN *raises her glass. Tempting. There are footsteps.*

BERNADETTE: [*offstage*] It would be nice to have a sit-down meal for Nan.

SEBASTIAN: Change the subject.

BERNADETTE *and* MARIE *walk back in.*

DAWN: [*covering*] The lighthouse was built in 1878 and is about thirty-four metres high. She's a real beauty.

BERNADETTE: Right, now we can start eating.

DAWN: Thank you Bernadette for telling me when I can eat.
    Very good manners this one. Nan loves him. Would you like a drink, Izzy?

BERNADETTE *eyes* IZZY.

IZZY: Actually Dawn, I would love some passion pop.

BERNADETTE: Excuse me?

DAWN *passes the passion pop to* IZZY.

IZZY: Well I'm not part of this family—you made sure of that, so I don't have to follow the rules. I'm not sorry either. I'm my own man, Bernadette. A single man.

DAWN: A single man.

IZZY: A man taking control of his destiny.

DAWN: A man destined for great things.

BERNADETTE: You're an accountant who can't even plan a dinner.

IZZY: Well maybe my time is now.

DAWN: Here, here.

DAWN *toasts.*

SEBASTIAN *looks between* DAWN *and* BERNADETTE.

SEBASTIAN: Give me some passion pop. Love you Dettie but I've never been a rule follower. And you'll always remain my favourite sister.

MARIE: Lovely.

BERNADETTE: Nan would be ashamed of all of you.

DAWN: She'd forgive us.

SEBASTIAN: It's what Catholics do.

BERNADETTE *looks at* MARIE. *Is she going to side with the others?*

MARIE: I'm with you.

DAWN: Maybe you two sad sacks should just fuck off a while. See the flat forehead friend. A party is starting.

MARIE: I wish I could go back to my flat forehead friend or even back to my family on the farm.

DAWN: *Your* family?

MARIE: You know what I meant.

DAWN: Oh I do, Marie. And I'll even raise a toast to it. Here's to family, your family Marie. How is your mother-in-law?

MARIE: If you must know, she's great.

DAWN: Yes, yes, that new family of yours is great. Better than us commoners.

MARIE: Don't be offensive.

DAWN: Still meet up with your mother-in-law every Friday for scones?

MARIE: She only lives fifty kilometres away. It's easier.

DAWN: Still, nice to be invited. I'll never know.

MARIE: Come then! Come Fridays for scones.

DAWN: Maybe I will.

MARIE: You won't. Because you never do. I asked you to the girls' christening and you didn't come.

DAWN: Darling, I was busy with Nan. You wouldn't want me there anyway. Not with your shiny new mother-in-law. She's the godmother, isn't she?

MARIE *glares at* DAWN, *not wanting to answer.*

Another toast then, Izzy.

IZZY: Okay.

DAWN: To new friends, to perfect godmothers, ungrateful kids, Nan—go to Jesus when you're ready, perhaps sooner if you can manage it. Here's to freedom and reconciliation.

IZZY: Freedom … and reconciliation.

IZZY, DAWN *and* SEBASTIAN *drink.*

BERNADETTE: Proving once again that this family has no healthy boundaries.

DAWN: Healthy boundaries? I think someone has been in therapy.

BERNADETTE: I read it in a book.

DAWN: One of them university books? Bernadette lording it over us with fancy words. She's better than us, everyone. She's come back from the east to lecture us all on healthy boundaries. That's probably all they do over there, talk about feelings.

IZZY: And house prices mostly.

BERNADETTE: I don't think I'm better than everyone else.

MARIE: You kind of do.

BERNADETTE: Marie, you're meant to be on my side.

MARIE: I am! But I'm not going to lie.

BERNADETTE: What is this? A mutiny?

DAWN: No mutinies here.

BERNADETTE: Just your typical nuthouse then.

DAWN: Nothing wrong with nuthouses.

BERNADETTE: You should know, right?

Awkward silence as everyone eats.

DAWN: You see what my daughter is trying to do there, Izzy? Shame me out. I admit it, I spent some time in the nuthouse. I was unfortunately in a state and my mother made me go. Several times in fact. The first time was just after I met Sebastian's dad—he was from Malta. Could do things with his tongue you wouldn't dream of.

SEBASTIAN: Oh Mum …

DAWN: And it was meant to be a fling but Catholic school doesn't teach you about contraception and what happens when you give into those natural urges of a teenage girl? Before I knew it I was knocked up and my Emmanuel was going back to Europe. I wasn't equipped to be a single mother. I mean, I love Sebastian but he was a mistake.

SEBASTIAN: You do so much for my self-esteem.

DAWN: But Nan, with her unnecessary and over the top devotion to our lord, forced me to stay with the nuns and living in that kind of humourless environment wasn't exactly thriving for a seventeen-year-old. Sister Helen called me a reincarnation of the devil and I spat in the grumpy old bat's face. What were you doing at seventeen, darling? I bet you were living a carefree existence, sculling tinnies, rooting around at the B and S ball in the back of a ute?

IZZY: I was graduating high school.

DAWN: Good for you. I'd always felt I hadn't lived. I'M A HOT-BLOODED WOMAN! But that brings shame on one's family and despite all the prayers the old girl and Sister Helen sent up there and after trying to jump off the roof of the church I was sent to the hospital and told that not even an exorcism would cure me. They certainly tried to zip those little blues away with their little contraptions. Just made me more of a nutter, I reckon. Would you like another piece of tuna mornay?

IZZY: Ummm …

DAWN: I'm not ashamed. I refuse to see shame in it. Do you see shame in it, Izzy?

IZZY: No. It's a sad story.

DAWN: Empathy. Do you have that fancy word in your city university book Bernadette? Does your mother-in-law use that word, Marie? Empathy anyone?

Awkward silence.

MARIE: I'll have some passion pop Mum.

DAWN: Good on you doll.

MARIE: I'm sorry Bernadette but this is a reminder of everything I don't want to be reminded of.

MARIE *pours herself a glass.*

Unbeknownst to everyone, NAN *sits up.*

BERNADETTE: I won't let you break me.

NAN *lies back down.*

DAWN: Are you on edge, Bernadette? Taking any pills, Bernadette?

BERNADETTE: No.

DAWN: Mummy knows. Izzy darling, would you like to hear a song?

IZZY: If it makes you happy.

DAWN: Yes it does make me happy. I'm fabulous at lip-syncing. Mum wouldn't let me sing in the choir so I learned early on to move my lips.

IZZY: I'm always keen for a show. [*To* BERNADETTE] You don't get to tell me what to do anymore.

DAWN *exits.* IZZY *sculls his drink.* NAN *sits up and puts on her glasses to read her clipboard. She places the clipboard back down, gets up and goes to the kitchen.*

BERNADETTE *sees* NAN *and is confused but brushes it off.*

DAWN: [*offstage*] Are we ready for me?

BERNADETTE: No.

IZZY: Yes.

SEBASTIAN: I'd have another scull.

DAWN: Sebastian.

SEBASTIAN: Fine.

MARIE: I need a top up.

BERNADETTE: I won't let her break me.

DAWN *walks out, wearing a feather boa from buy and sell. She's dressed up—tragically op shop. Interestingly she has no microphone but a dildo in its place. She turns on the record player and 'Delta Dawn' begins playing. She starts lip syncing.*

After the first verse, DAWN *picks up a donut and begins mimicking the dildo going in the hole as she lip syncs.*

NAN *comes back from the kitchen with a glass of water and a book.* BERNADETTE *watches her get into bed.* BERNADETTE *thinks she's going mad.*

SEBASTIAN: Fuck it. I'm joining in.

SEBASTIAN *starts singing.*

MARIE *shrugs, she joins in too.* IZZY *doesn't know whether to clap along or not.* BERNADETTE *pulls the plug to the record machine.*

BERNADETTE: Are you all fucking kidding me?

DAWN: Ugh. Take a chill pill.

DAWN *throws the donut at* BERNADETTE.

It triggers BERNADETTE.

BERNADETTE: Good idea.

BERNADETTE *digs through a draw and pulls out a bottle of pills.*

DAWN *runs around* NAN *as* BERNADETTE *chases her.* SEBASTIAN *tries to calm everyone down.* MARIE *continues filling her glass.*

NAN *continues reading.*

IZZY *stands up.*

BERNADETTE *tackles* DAWN *to the ground.*

DAWN: What are you doing to me?

BERNADETTE: Marie get her legs. Sebastian hold her arms. These are healthy boundaries!

SEBASTIAN: Sorry Mummy.

Everyone is holding DAWN. IZZY *watches on in horror.* NAN *gets up and stands next to* IZZY. *He does a double-take.*

IZZY: Nan?

Everyone stops and looks at NAN *standing there.* NAN *realises that they are shocked to see her.*

NAN: Oh. Only funnin'. I was a little bit thirsty.

SEBASTIAN: Nan!

MARIE: Nan!

MARIE *and* SEBASTIAN *jump up and hug* NAN.

DAWN *is still on the ground.*

BERNADETTE: Shit! Marie call the doctor. Sebastian get her water. Izzy go get her meds bag.

MARIE, SEBASTIAN *and* IZZY *exit.*

NAN: Where am I?

BERNADETTE: At home.

NAN: Oh I thought I was dead.

BERNADETTE: We thought so too!

DAWN *slumps further down.*

SEBASTIAN *rushes back in with water.*

SEBASTIAN: We prayed really, really hard. I knew it wasn't your time.

NAN: They only take the good ones.

NAN *drinks the water and sits back in her bed.*

MARIE *rushes in with the phone.*

MARIE: The doctor can't believe it.

SEBASTIAN: You should call the priest too.

MARIE: For what?

SEBASTIAN: Let them know they got a win!

DAWN *groans in the background.*

BERNADETTE: Sebastian, get Mum some water. Sober her up.

SEBASTIAN *gets more water.*

MARIE: Everything can go back to normal!

BERNADETTE: We still need to get her checked.

MARIE: Doesn't matter, she's back.

DAWN *groans again.*

NAN: What on earth is that noise?

BERNADETTE: Don't worry about buggalugs there.

SEBASTIAN *walks in with water and a flannel for* DAWN.

SEBASTIAN: And a cold flannel for you, Mummy.

DAWN: [*more coherently*] What happened?

SEBASTIAN: Good news! Nanny's back.

DAWN: Ugh! Fuck!

SEBASTIAN *puts the flannel on* DAWN*'s head.*

The three grandchildren surround Nan's bed.

BERNADETTE: How do you feel?

NAN: Like I just came back from the dead.

SEBASTIAN: Did you see heaven?

NAN: Unfortunately not.

MARIE: What did you see?

NAN: Dreams of … The Batavia funnily enough.

MARIE: Oh, Bernadette's favourite subject.

BERNADETTE: We're all here now.

NAN: Dying is the only way I get to see you lot.

MARIE: You know you can just call and ask us to come see you.

NAN: But you still won't move back home.

SEBASTIAN: Don't worry Nanny … I'll move back. And I'm going to marry Mary-Ann.

MARIE: What?

SEBASTIAN: I made a promise.

NAN: Which one was Mary-Ann again?

SEBASTIAN *goes to say 'cock mouth'.*

SEBASTIAN: She had a slight c—

BERNADETTE: Do not say it.

SEBASTIAN: The point is I'm moving back.

NAN: No you can stay over there … My grandson is the opera star. No. Marie and Bernadette can move back.

BERNADETTE: We're just happy you're here.

IZZY *walks in with bags.*

NAN: Are you a doctor?

IZZY: No I'm an accountant, actually.

NAN: Oh I don't have any money.

IZZY: I was told to get your meds bag but I didn't know which one was it and so I just grabbed every bag in the house.

NAN: I thought accountants just did taxes.

BERNADETTE *goes to* IZZY.

BERNADETTE: What the hell?

IZZY: I panicked.

BERNADETTE: That's not the meds bag. It's the brown one, with the stripe.

IZZY: What coloured stripe?

BERNADETTE: Red or white.

IZZY: There wasn't a brown one with a red or white stripe. I checked.

BERNADETTE: You didn't look hard enough.

IZZY: I did.

BERNADETTE *gives him the eye.* IZZY *feels guilty again.*

I'm sorry. I'll go look.

BERNADETTE: Thank you.

BERNADETTE *goes back to* NAN.

NAN: How many times I got to die to get a tea around here.

MARIE: I got it!

NAN: And my glasses!

SEBASTIAN: I got it.

MARIE *and* SEBASTIAN *exit.*

NAN *exhales a big breath.*

BERNADETTE: Rest easy.

NAN *looks lovingly at* BERNADETTE.

NAN: You came home.

BERNADETTE: You said I could always come back.

NAN: My sweet grandchild. How did you become the brightest of stars amongst the darkness?

BERNADETTE: Don't leave again. I'll go check on that tea.

BERNADETTE *exits.*

DAWN: It's nice when you get all the attention, isn't it, Mum?

NAN: Oh shush. You've been gallivanting about town no doubt while I've been comatose.

DAWN: Gallivanting is living. Just because you didn't live life as it was intended. Big bursts of energy, like a wild storm, charging through. Changing things up.

NAN: Every storm whimpers out.

DAWN: Life can't be experienced through a window, Mum.

NAN: Of course it can. You have books, you have television, you have a view of the lighthouse.

DAWN: The lighthouse. How exciting! Look at it just turning, cycling and doing sweet fuck all. A bit like you.

NAN: I don't tolerate profanity.

DAWN: I had everything organised until Bernadette came. Then she got upset because I serenaded her ex-fiancé with a dildo.

NAN: What's a dildo?

DAWN: You stick it up your twat for pleasure.

NAN: Pass the rosary beads.

DAWN: Did you meet your God? Did you tell him about the lighthouse? I don't care if you are here for good. I'm out of this morgue with the fairy lights.

NAN: You may not believe it Dawn, but I pray for forgiveness every day. My failures as a mother, my failures as a Catholic. I tried to come to your side but I couldn't step out of that door. Fear ruled me and despite praying for better health, for peace, for a swim at the beach under the glow of the lighthouse, I could not will myself out. Only death will set me free of that curse.

DAWN: Let's go then Mummy. Let's go for a swim right now! Skinny dipping even!

NAN: Don't be daft. I'm convalescing.

DAWN *is frustrated.*

DAWN: Even when faced with death you won't have a tiny bit of pleasure.

NAN: Dawn come here. I acknowledge it's my fault you are the way you are.

DAWN: That'll be a first.

NAN: But those children need stability …

DAWN: The children you turned against me?

NAN: They need stability. You need stability. No gallivanting, no skulduggery and no tomfoolery.

NAN *pats the bed and* DAWN *gets into the bed with* NAN.

DAWN: Do you pray for me Mum?

NAN: Every second. Every hour. Every day. As constant as the lighthouse. What did you call this town?

DAWN: A morgue with fairy lights.

NAN *smiles.*

NAN: When Bernadette gets back, tell her to tell me the Batavia story. If there's one regret I have, it's missing that.

They fall asleep.

SCENE TEN—A PLANNED MUTINY

MARIE *walks in searching for her flask.* IZZY *comes in.*

IZZY: I can't find the bag. Bernadette's going to kill me. And … smell that …

MARIE: What?

IZZY *takes three sniffs.* MARIE *sniffs.*

IZZY: It's coming … It's coming from … Smells like … Smells like … marijuana! On you!

MARIE *can't deny it.*

MARIE: It's not a crime.

IZZY: Pretty sure it is.

MARIE: So what … I found some of my old stash in my room and decided to light up in my car while listening to soft rock. I'm enjoying myself.

IZZY: To soft rock?

MARIE: I needed a little me time. I don't get me time anymore. I'm an awful mother. You're going to report me.

IZZY: To authorities?

MARIE: To my family. They'll laugh—'oh the ice queen', don't think I don't know they call me that, 'the ice queen that hands pamphlets out for John Trudgett'.

IZZY: The racist senator?

MARIE: You don't know the pressure. The farm. The kids. The mothers. I get up at five am and make cupcakes for daycare Monday, Wednesday and Friday. And then Danielle says her child is lactose intolerant. I have to change recipes. Never mind I have to tend to two crying kids who won't latch onto my nipples. And my mother-in-law helicopters … around me. I have to be the perfect mother, perfect wife, perfect daughter-in-law. I promised myself to never abandon my kids, not even for a night. It wasn't going to be like my childhood. I was going to smother them … with love.

IZZY: Thank God you finished that sentence.

MARIE: Bernadette said everything can go back to normal but I don't want to go back to that normal. I don't want to go home. So yeah, I smoked marijuana and listened to soft rock and it was the best time I've had in years.

IZZY: Have you thought of therapy?

MARIE: No way. I'm perfectly sane.

IZZY: When Bernadette is in therapy—

MARIE: Bernadette's in therapy?

IZZY: Was.

MARIE: I knew it!

IZZY: Please don't say anything.

MARIE: [*delightedly*] She's crazy.

> MARIE *runs into the room.*

IZZY: I'd say it runs in the family.

> DAWN *wakes up and sees* IZZY …

DAWN: Izzy—buzzzz, buzzzz, buzzzz.

> IZZY *looks around trying to work out where the buzzing came from.*

Izzy … bzzzzz.

> IZZY *finally sees* DAWN. DAWN *gets up and goes to the door. She gestures him to come over.*

I have a light bulb out in my caravan. Might I borrow your strong arms?

> IZZY *considers it. He shrugs.*

IZZY: Yeah sure.

> IZZY *follows* DAWN *offstage.*

SCENE ELEVEN—A PRAYER FOR DAVY JONES' LOCKER

SEBASTIAN *walks in, on his phone. He looks around. No-one is around. He takes a photo of down his pants.*

BERNADETTE: [*offstage*] Marie!

> SEBASTIAN *hides his phone.* MARIE *comes running in. Followed by* BERNADETTE.

MARIE: She went to see a therapist.

SEBASTIAN: A real one? Not just one with crystals like Mum tried in 2002.

BERNADETTE: A crystal therapist is a white woman venture … like our mother.

MARIE: So you saw a real one.

BERNADETTE: I'm gonna kill Izzy. Where is he?

SEBASTIAN: We had a pact.

MARIE: Yes, we had a pact.

BERNADETTE: What pact?

SEBASTIAN: No therapists.

MARIE: No psychologists.

SEBASTIAN: No psychiatrists.

SEBASTIAN *and* MARIE: [*together*] Never, never talk about the curse.

SEBASTIAN: Or we'll end up like Mum.

MARIE: Getting committed. You're getting committed aren't you?

SEBASTIAN: Or are *we* getting committed?

BERNADETTE: I didn't say a thing.

SEBASTIAN: What? You went there and sat in silence. Had a cup of tea?

MARIE: Scones? Jam and cream.

SEBASTIAN: Sitting with tea, scones with jam and cream!

BERNADETTE: That's not how therapy works.

MARIE: So you did say things?

BERNADETTE: Maybe I needed outside advice on things.

MARIE: You could have asked us.

SEBASTIAN: Yeah, we're family.

BERNADETTE: What makes us family? Politics? Our fathers? It's not like we even look like each other.

SEBASTIAN: That's never been an issue. We're still the same blood.

BERNADETTE: You all drive me crazy.

MARIE: So what? You're abandoning ship?

BERNADETTE: This ship is wrecked.

> IZZY *walks in. He looks a little flustered.*

IZZY: Bernadette. Can I talk to you a second?

BERNADETTE: I don't have a second. You told my business to my sister.

MARIE: Are you saying you're not looking after Mum?

BERNADETTE: What if I am?

SEBASTIAN: No, no, no, no.

MARIE: [*to* SEBASTIAN] This is your fault.

> *All hell breaks loose.* BERNADETTE, IZZY, MARIE *and* SEBASTIAN *yell at the same time.*

BERNADETTE: You had no right to tell my brother and sister. No right whatsoever. You always sticking your big black nostrils where they don't belong. It's none of your business. So don't come here pretending that you're the saviour. You have no idea what I do.

IZZY: I didn't mean to tell your sister. Not that you would listen to my side of the story because I'm always in the wrong according to you. There's nothing wrong with therapy. Of course you don't like to let anyone in. But I actually need to tell you something else.

MARIE: Selfish. You're the one that left the country, Sebastian. You're the one that abandoned ship. You left us with this whole mess. And you swan back in here with your fake stories, pretending everything is fine and now you're surprised that nothing is fine. So fucking typical of you. No wonder I want to leave.

SEBASTIAN: You're the one who is selfish Marie. You can't stand that Bernadette and me have gone out into the world and tried to make something of ourselves while you jumped into the tractor with the first farmer you see, which by the way was your choice. Busting yourself to get a new family.

During the fight DAWN *walks in wearing a feather boa with a Woman's Day cocktail and sits down on the lounge as her kids continue arguing. She redoes her lipstick. The argument ends on:*

BERNADETTE: SHUT UP!

MARIE: What?

BERNADETTE: I hear it.

SEBASTIAN: What?

BERNADETTE: I can hear the rattles. Mum, Nan's not funning this time.

This is news to DAWN.

SEBASTIAN: But … I'm not ready.

BERNADETTE: None of us are.

MARIE: What do we do?

BERNADETTE: Pray.

DAWN: I better clean up.

IZZY: Bernadette, can I talk to you?

BERNADETTE: Not now, I'm praying.

BERNADETTE, SEBASTIAN *and* MARIE *sit beside* NAN.

IZZY: I need to talk to you Bernadette.

DAWN *closes the windows.*

SEBASTIAN: Everyone hold hands.

They bow their heads. MARIE *reluctantly.*

SEBASTIAN *clears his throat.*

Hail Mary … full of grace.

He can't think what the next words are.

Full of grace … Hail Mary.

MARIE: You said that already.

DAWN *re-opens the windows. She wipes them clean.*

SEBASTIAN: I can't remember it.

MARIE: You were an altar boy.

SEBASTIAN: I spent most of my time stealing wine for Mum.

DAWN *starts sweeping the ceiling.*

Hail Mary, full of grace.

MARIE: Full of grace.

SEBASTIAN: Full of grace!

MARIE: Stop repeating.

SEBASTIAN: Hail Mary full of grace ...

DAWN: The Lord is with thee. Blessed art thou amongst women, and blessed is the fruit of thy womb, Jesus. Holy Mary, Mother of God, pray for us sinners, now and at the hour of our death. Amen. [*Off everyone's look*] I said a lot of rosaries for penance. Now can we please clean!

IZZY: Bernadette.

BERNADETTE: Not now! Everyone say your goodbyes.

MARIE: Nan, if I had my time over again, I wouldn't have smoked that joint in my car.

BERNADETTE: Marijuana?

SEBASTIAN: Oh my God.

MARIE: I'm gonna say it ... Here it comes. I love you Nan.

SEBASTIAN: Really?

MARIE: I've said I love you before.

SEBASTIAN: I don't think I've ever heard you say I love you.

BERNADETTE: Sebastian. Your turn.

SEBASTIAN *grabs* NAN*'s hand.*

SEBASTIAN: Nan, it was an honour being your grandson. Every time I sing, I'll sing in your name—up to the heavens. Where angels and doves fly.

DAWN *exits and reappears with the vacuum cleaner.*

And ... And ... And I'm gay.

MARIE: You announce you're gay on Nan's dying breath?

SEBASTIAN: Izzy said I'd regret not saying it.

IZZY: I did say that.

SEBASTIAN: I'm sorry I can't marry Mariann Cock Mouth.

IZZY: But not that.

MARIE: Jesus! I say *I love you* for the first time and you out do me with 'cock in your mouth'.

BERNADETTE: Really? This is what you want Nan's last moments on earth to be … talking about cock, Sebastian, and your drugs, Marie?

SEBASTIAN: Cock mouth actually. [*Off* BERNADETTE*'s look*] Okay you go.

BERNADETTE: Mum … ! Mum!

It's time.

DAWN: I've already said my goodbyes.

NAN *takes a strained breath.* BERNADETTE *leads* DAWN *to* NAN. *She sits by her side.* NAN *prepares to take her last final breath … She breathes in. Everyone breathes with her … This is it. This is the time.*

Beat.

Everyone is in shock. What is going to happen? They look to BERNADETTE *for direction.*

BERNADETTE: The most important thing is we need to stick together right now. We live life like Nan wanted us too—cooperatively, balanced, truthful. Healthy boundaries.

IZZY *can't hold it in anymore.*

IZZY: Dawn kissed me.

BERNADETTE: We're fucked.

Blackout.

END OF ACT ONE

ACT TWO

SCENE ONE—A QUESTION OF NEW TERRITORY

'What's your Mama's Name, Child' by Tanya Tucker starts playing.

It's funeral day.

And where are our characters at?

SEBASTIAN *pours some passion pop into a flask, occasionally taking swigs from the bottle. He pulls out his anxiety pills. He washes them down with more passion pop.*

MARIE *is smoking yarndi. Just what she needed. She blows out the smoke and shoos it away. She sprays perfume on her neck, wrists and under her skirts for good luck.*

BERNADETTE *and* IZZY *are getting dressed post-moonyin (post-sex).* BERNADETTE *slips on a black dress.* IZZY *does up his pants' fly. No words are spoken—that's how unemotional it was.*

Everyone steps forward dressed in black and ready for the funeral.

And the grand entrance ... DAWN, *giant funeral hat, tight funeral dress (which emphasises her cleavage), gloves, handkerchief. She walks downstage to deliver her eulogy.* BERNADETTE, IZZY, SEBASTIAN *and* MARIE *stand listening.* SEBASTIAN *and* MARIE *are both uncomfortable.* BERNADETTE *is apathetic to it all.*

DAWN: My mother Valda Dawn Osborn was as part of this town as the red and white stripes of the lighthouse, as a bag of one dollar tomatoes, as the Southerly, blowing its guts out. Her and her sister Mildred overcame many hardships in their lives thanks to their strong faith in God and rejection of tomfoolery and skulduggery like the rest of this town. Sure it made her a little boring, a bit of shut in but Val was a good Catholic and let's face it ... good Catholics are hard to find nowadays. I'm not exaggerating when I say she was a patron saint of the selfless. She helped me raise three children ... when I wasn't ... able to ... and I'm forever grateful. Sure, one's a drug addict, one's homosexual and one's in therapy but Mother did her best and held this family together like a stitching to a wound. But she's finally free of this sinful world, closer to God, judging us all, like she always wanted. Ashes to ashes, dust to dust.

Beat.

Now if you'll join me for the wake at the local watering hole. I will be performing a dance routine to ABBA's 'Dancing Queen' followed by 'The Winner Takes It All'. Open bar.

MARIE: [*to* BERNADETTE] Are you going to stop her? Or are we just going to witness this ship sinking?

BERNADETTE *considers the question.*

SEBASTIAN, MARIE, IZZY *and* DAWN *exit.*

BERNADETTE *puts on a flowered lanyard.*

The southerly starts to blow hard. BERNADETTE *begins to realise her nan is gone.*

SCENE TWO—SHIPWRECKED

Inside Nan's house.

BERNADETTE *picks up a box. It contains Nan's ashes. It's a cheap box—* BERNADETTE *probably doesn't even realise it contains* NAN. *She puts the box on the piano.*

She pulls an envelope from her bra that's already been opened. She unfolds the letter and reads it. Not good news. She pulls out a cigarette and lighter and she burns the letter with the lighter.

She pulls out a flask and takes a swig and a couple of antidepressants. She doesn't give a fuck anymore.

BERNADETTE *adjusts herself.*

She pulls out a moving box and starts packing.

MARIE *and* SEBASTIAN *enter.*

BERNADETTE: The fucking state government approved plans to bulldoze this place and build a hotel.

SEBASTIAN: Wait what?

MARIE: It does have the best views of the lighthouse.

SEBASTIAN: You're not angry?

MARIE: Don't you remember those six-monthly government inspections where they told us the skirting boards were dusty or the oven wasn't clean enough? Government letters to Nan with the 'it's come to our attention that you have family members living there that are not on the lease' or 'your rent is overdue by two days', and that bright yellow sticker with 'please pay at your earliest convenience, yours sincerely'. They actually highlighted our poverty for us. This was never our home. Bulldoze away. Set sail from this place of misery.

SEBASTIAN: Yeah but remember all the Christmases, birthdays, Easters, Sunday roast cooked from scratch. First day of school photos by the tree out the back, first broken arm by jumping off the bed, first hand job in the back … shed. Look—see this mark here. This happened when I hid match heads in Pop's cigarette and told him to light it. He chased me down the street calling me a mongrel bastard. Good memories. This is our home.

MARIE: Then why did you leave?

SEBASTIAN: Because we could always come back.

Beat.

So should we tell Mum it's getting knocked down? Or wait for a better time?

MARIE: It's the perfect time. Mum and Aunt Mildred are outside discussing why Cousin Kerry's potato salad is blasphemous.

SEBASTIAN: I bet it's the fennel that throws them. I can't do it. Mum's giving me the silent treatment. I thought I'd enjoy the peace but being back around Catholics reminds me how I can't enjoy anything.

MARIE: At least she didn't brand you a drug addict in front of the five people at the funeral.

BERNADETTE: I'll do it. I'll talk to Mum.

       BERNADETTE *walks out leaving* MARIE *and* SEBASTIAN *concerned.*

MARIE: I think she's planning something.

SEBASTIAN: What?

MARIE: Mutiny.

       SEBASTIAN *and* MARIE *exit.*

SCENE THREE—ABANDON SHIP

MILDRED *and* DAWN *walk into the house and sit at the table. They are sharing a pot of tea and mock chicken sandwiches.*

MILDRED: They've been terrorising the street for a month now. I wake up and my driveway is a mess. Rubbish everywhere. Poor Vern has to clean it all up and he's had a bad back for years. It's only making it worse. Doctor O'Brien said he shouldn't be lifting. I'm at my wits' end. Criminals. I even called the police, you think they'd do anything. Pfff. They said it's not a police matter.

DAWN: That's bloody terrible Aunt Mildred.

MILDRED: This is the state of the world today. Can't be safe in our own homes from those terrorists. And they know it. I caught one the other day on our roof. Sitting up there, taunting us. I yelled at him to get off, but he just sat there in defiance.

DAWN: Oh no. What happened?

MILDRED: He took a big shit. On our roof. Staring at us in the eye. That's how they treat us. Shitting and staring at us.

> DAWN *is shocked.*

DAWN: Something really needs to be done about those ibis birds.

> MILDRED *spills her sandwich.*

MILDRED: Oh the devil.

DAWN: Not to worry. Da da da da!

> DAWN *gets out a dust-buster. She vacuums up the sandwich crumbs.*

There see?

> BERNADETTE *walks in.*

Got it off buy and sell. Bargain. They even took a couple of dollars off when I showed up in my funeral gear this morning.

MILDRED: With the hat?

DAWN: I'm thinking of wearing it to IGA. Imagine the sympathy discounts off cold cuts.

> DAWN *laughs. She spots* BERNADETTE.

BERNADETTE: Dawn!

DAWN: Don't worry. No fun being had in here. You made sure of that by stopping jello shots at the wake.

> MARIE *and* SEBASTIAN *enter carrying boxes.*

BERNADETTE: We need to talk.

SEBASTIAN: Hi Mummy.

DAWN: [*ignoring* SEBASTIAN] I'm in mourning.

BERNADETTE: The state government has sold this land to developers.

> BERNADETTE *looks at* DAWN.

DAWN: Aunt Mildred would you like another mock chicken sandwich?

BERNADETTE: Jesus. Are you listening to me?

DAWN: Don't take the Lord's name in vain. This is a holy house.

MILDRED: Actually I'll have a cocktail.

DAWN: Unfortunately all alcohol was banned from the house after an unfortunate incident with the fun police. Can't even make you a cocktail.

> MILDRED *pulls out a bottle of whiskey from her purse.*

MILDRED: Lucky I brought my own.

DAWN: I thought that was whiskey straight.

> MILDRED *shakes it.*

MILDRED: Now it's a cocktail.

> DAWN *laughs.*

DAWN: I'll get you some ice.

MILDRED: Have you got any large glasses?

> DAWN *exits to the kitchen,* MILDRED *follows.*

BERNADETTE: She can't ignore it forever. She has two weeks.

SEBASTIAN: Did you see how she ignored me. I can't take being on the outer. Is this what it's like, Marie?

MARIE: She's not angry at you because you're gay. She's angry because she's missed out on twenty years of Mardi Gras and telling everyone who will listen that she has a gay son. That's the biggest sin of all.

SEBASTIAN: Oh God. She'd be the first one on the allied float, with her tits out and a thong on. Her drag name would be something like …

BERNADETTE, SEBASTIAN *and* MARIE: [*together*] Horny Dawny.

IZZY *arrives wearing a Bintang singlet, board shorts and Oakley sunglasses, holding two bags of tomatoes.*

IZZY: Did you know you can get a whole bag of tomatoes ... A whole bag ... for one dollar. ONE DOLLAR! I bought twenty bags ... for twenty dollars. I've been sightseeing.

MARIE: To the tomato stall?

IZZY: When in Rome.

SEBASTIAN: You know Rome has a colosseum, Sistine Chapel, beautiful men ... Geraldton has a tomato stall.

IZZY: I can't believe you don't appreciate this place. Beaches, sunshine. It's the lifestyle here.

SEBASTIAN: Oh God he's assimilating. Who gave you those God awful clothes?

IZZY: Your mum. Belonged to some alcoholic cousin?

MARIE *and* SEBASTIAN: [*together*] Cousin Merve.

IZZY: Where's he now?

MARIE *and* SEBASTIAN: [*together*] Dead.

IZZY: Alcohol poisoning?

BERNADETTE *discretely takes another antidepressant.*

SEBASTIAN: No, choked on a ham bone from one of Aunt Mildred's pea soups. Rumour is she did it on purpose.

IZZY: That nice little lady?

MARIE: She clutched her bag as you walked past her at the wake.

BERNADETTE: Who cares about cousin Merve and Aunt Mildred and possible homicide. Let's get packing.

SEBASTIAN *and* MARIE *start grabbing boxes.*

IZZY: I got you tomatoes. It was the best-looking bag there. Very firm. I think you'll be impressed.

BERNADETTE *ignores* IZZY.

BERNADETTE: I'm busy.

She continues packing.

IZZY: What are we doing?

BERNADETTE: *We* are packing the house up.

IZZY: Oh good. I can help. I was a removalist back during uni. I even know the bending technique.

IZZY does a flirty bend. MARIE *and* SEBASTIAN *tilt their heads, impressed. But* BERNADETTE *isn't impressed.*

BERNADETTE: What are you doing?

IZZY: Trying to make you smile.

BERNADETTE: It's my grandmother's funeral today.

IZZY: All the more reason to try and make you smile.

BERNADETTE: Don't you have a flight back to Sydney?

IZZY: But we … I thought things had been resolved with us. You [*noticing* MARIE *and* SEBASTIAN *watching*] came to me and we resolved everything. Didn't we?

MARIE *and* SEBASTIAN *pretend to look elsewhere.*

BERNADETTE *doesn't know how to answer.*

BERNADETTE: I need to pack.

In walks MILDRED *and* DAWN.

MILDRED: You spit into a tube, send it off and from your spit they can tell what exotic corner of the wide world your ancestors came from. Got the results back last week. One hundred per cent poor English. I was hoping for something a little more exotic … like Scottish.

DAWN: How fascinating. Did you hear that? We're all English.

BERNADETTE, SEBASTIAN, MARIE *and* IZZY *exchange a look.*

SEBASTIAN: That's why I'm miserable all the time.

DAWN: Izzy darl! How was the sightseeing?

IZZY: I got tomatoes.

DAWN: You beaut! Doesn't he look like cousin Merve, Aunt Mildred?

MILDRED: Such a shame about Merve.

SEBASTIAN *and* MARIE *share a sideways look.*

DAWN: Izzy, have a mock chicken sandwich. I saved them for you.

IZZY *tries to keep distance between him and* DAWN.

IZZY: Actually I've got to pack.

DAWN: Don't be silly, it's a day of mourning. Give those broad shoulders of yours a rest. Doesn't he have broad shoulders, Aunt Mildred?

MILDRED: I can't see that far.

IZZY: Oh, I have the opposite to broad, narrow.

BERNADETTE: Have you two finished?

DAWN: I'm just having a conversation about shoulders Bernadette. All innocent.

SEBASTIAN: I have shoulders too, Mummy.

DAWN: Too narrow.

BERNADETTE: Sebastian take one room, Marie take another. Only essentials are to be kept and the rubbish pile is over here.

IZZY: I'll help Sebastian!

> MARIE, SEBASTIAN *and* IZZY *disperse.*

DAWN: You've poisoned everyone against me.

BERNADETTE: This is not going to be a difficult process. I'm in charge now and first thing is first, you're back on your meds.

DAWN: I'm already on my meds.

BERNADETTE: I wasn't born yesterday. I counted them last week. I counted them this morning. You haven't taken any.

DAWN: You sound like your grandmother. Maybe I get more done in a state.

BERNADETTE: I don't buy that excuse anymore.

DAWN: Well maybe I want to mourn my mother. Feel her gone from this house. Have a proper fucking process. She was a saint! Isn't that right, Aunt Mildred?

MILDRED: What was that?

DAWN: [*loudly*] That your sister was a saint? A saint for the selfless.

> MILDRED *considers.*

MILDRED: Any chance of a top up?

> *Mildred's phone starts ringing.* DAWN *tops her up.*

BERNADETTE: Take them, or I'll call in a doctor and they'll make you. And no more whiskey for Mildred.

DAWN: Aunt Mildred's in mourning.

MILDRED: Oh it's probably Vern. Probably looking for his curried egg sandwich. [*Shouting into the phone—Uncle Vern is deaf*] HELLO.

BERNADETTE: Send her home. Nan banned Aunt Mildred from the house years ago.

DAWN: She was only banned from Christmas lunches.

BERNADETTE: Because she was an old drunk.

MILDRED: [*into the phone*] NO, IN THE FRIDGE, LOVE. WHAT DO YOU MEAN YOU CAN'T OPEN IT?

BERNADETTE: And she always ends up insulting Nan or myself, or Marie or Sebastian.

DAWN: There's nothing she could insult Sebastian for? Except maybe now he's a gay.

MILDRED: [*into the phone*] FOR GOODNESS SAKE, DON'T PUT YOUR BACK OUT AGAIN.

MARIE, SEBASTIAN *(wearing a kimono he's found) and* IZZY *walk back in with boxes. They start sorting through them, throwing things into the rubbish pile. They have a different conversation. It's family chaos.*

MARIE: [*to* SEBASTIAN] Are you wearing our dead grandmother's kimono?

SEBASTIAN: I like the feel on my skin.

BERNADETTE: [*to* DAWN] It would be nice if you were this protective of your children instead of some alcoholic racist Aunt.

DAWN: I don't know why you insist on this crusade of perfection, Bernadette. You come back from the east wanting to change everything.

BERNADETTE: And what's wrong with that?

MILDRED: [*into the phone*] DON'T GO BACK TO MASSAGE, YOU'LL JUST MAKE IT WORSE. LIKE YOUR PROSTATE.

SEBASTIAN *flicks through a magazine.*

DAWN: People are happy here. It's a simple life. No complications. No daylight savings. Everyone works hard and nobody is offended.

MILDRED: [*into the phone*] WELL GO ASK THAT CHINAMAN TO FIX IT.

Everyone stops.

DAWN: He probably is a man from China. She's from an era.

BERNADETTE: A really racist era.

IZZY: Is this normal?

MARIE: She once told second cousin Enid at Great Uncle Ted's seventieth that I was responsible for World War Two.

DAWN: Be considerate, Marie. Our great-great uncle was held by the Japanese and Aunt Mildred took it personally.

MARIE: I'm not from Japan.

DAWN: Yeah well, Asia is a big country.

BERNADETTE: Continent.

DAWN: You and your fancy words. Aunt Mildred loves everyone deep down. She's a Catholic. Don't tell her about Sebastian being a gay.

SEBASTIAN: And I'll take this off.

SEBASTIAN *takes off the kimono.*

MILDRED: [*into the phone*] OH YOU'RE HOPELESS VERN, A BLOODY IDIOT. I'VE GOT TO GO. How do I turn this thing off?

DAWN *goes over and helps her.* DAWN *pulls out a baby wipe and cleans the screen.*

He was opening the fridge the wrong way. Hopeless.

DAWN: All that pulling, probably made his back worse!

MILDRED: He's an idiot. Hasn't been right in the head since he went to the Korean war.

MILDRED *stops and looks at* MARIE. DAWN *intervenes.*

DAWN: Let me fix that drink Aunt Mildred.

DAWN *tops her up.*

SEBASTIAN: Talk about something else before the room blows.

IZZY: What do you want done with the piano?

SEBASTIAN: Good one. That's a keep.

BERNADETTE: I'm selling it.

SEBASTIAN: What?

MARIE: Are you sure?

DAWN: Blasphemy.

SEBASTIAN: That's Nan's pride and joy.

BERNADETTE: And Nan isn't here anymore. None of us play anymore.

SEBASTIAN: I play.

BERNADETTE: Are you going to ship it to Portugal?

SEBASTIAN: Marie will take it.

MARIE: It doesn't go with my furniture.

SEBASTIAN: [*to* IZZY] You had to bring up the piano.

IZZY: It was just a question to redirect from the racist aunt.

MILDRED: I remember when Val bought that piano. She always wanted one. Ever since she was a little kid. But we grew up dirt poor, couldn't afford shoes let alone a piano. Val had trouble fitting in, she had the nerves from a young age. And then she heard our neighbour playing. Old Mr Murphy, good Catholic, but a bit strange, possibly touched, back then it was a blue light disco with the altar boys after mass. But she went over there every morning and afternoon and learnt how to play. I told her she was never going to make a good wife playing the piano, she needed to learn how to cook and sew. When she married your father, Dawn, I said to her that she can kiss her piano dreams goodbye. He was poorer than us! And what money he had from the railways, he would spend it at the pub or on the gee-gees. But Val would wait until your father would come home inebriated and raid his pockets for coins. Wasn't long until she had the full lot. Even for the shipping from Perth. There's only been two days I've seen Val happy and one was the day her piano arrived.

BERNADETTE: What was the other?

MILDRED: Pardon?

BERNADETTE: What was the other time she was happy?

MILDRED: When the Queen came to Geraldton.

DAWN: So the day I was born then! Ha!

MILDRED: No love. When the Queen came to Geraldton.

MARIE: Well now I definitely don't want the piano. Imagine looking at Nan's betrayal and disappointment for us not following through every day.

DAWN: Poor Val, this family is falling apart since she departed us and now her grandkids want to get rid of the one symbol that kept her going when all of youse left her.

Everyone is silent.

IZZY: I think I'll go start on the shed.

Avoiding DAWN, IZZY *exits.*

MARIE: Why don't you keep it Bernadette?

BERNADETTE: Why would I?

MARIE: Because you were the best. Nan was always saying how you played 'Fur Elise' the best.

BERNADETTE: I hate Beethoven.

DAWN *digs through the rubbish pile.*

BERNADETTE *moves over to the piano. She runs her finger over the keys. Memories surface with every touch. She starts to feel the loss of Nan.*

MARIE: Bernadette?

BERNADETTE *starts to breathe heavily. Something is wrong.*

SEBASTIAN: Dettie?

BERNADETTE: In 1629 the Batavia started ... voyage ... shipwreck ... One hundred and ten ... men ... women ... and ... children.

MARIE: What's wrong with her?

BERNADETTE: Nothing. I just, lost my breath.

DAWN *lets out a scream. Even* MILDRED *spills her drink in fright.*

[*Concernedly*] What?

DAWN: Why have you thrown these out? These are my limited editions of *Woman's Day!* They're not rubbish. They have Diana in it.

SEBASTIAN: Oh Saint Diana.

DAWN: She *was* a saint.

MARIE: The people's princess.

DAWN: I relate to her. We're both divorcees with good fashion taste and families that try to kill us. So why do I have to get rid of my special edition *Woman's Day?*

BERNADETTE *cracks it.*

BERNADETTE: Because they have to go. Because I'm in charge. Because I'm giving up my life to take care of you. Because you forever need looking after. Because you can't be trusted. Because you kissed my man!

Everyone stops. IZZY *walks back in, and walks back out.*

MILDRED: Think I'm going to need a stronger drink.

DAWN: I'm going to my van. Aunt Mildred care to join me?

MILDRED: What van?

DAWN: I'm going to Adelaide.

MILDRED: There's a van in Adelaide?

DAWN: Aunt Mildred, come outside away from these horrible people.

SEBASTIAN: Look Pop's old CDs! Maybe this will make time go quicker.

MARIE: Or at least distract from the excruciating awkwardness.

BERNADETTE: We should drink.

BERNADETTE *takes a swig of Mildred's whiskey. She searches for where she's hidden a bottle of passion pop.*

Care to join me. La la la la la.

MARIE *thinks. She takes a swig of passion pop.*

SEBASTIAN *inserts the CD and presses play.*

And give me some …

MARIE: What?

BERNADETTE: I know you have some.

MARIE *reluctantly pulls out a joint, lights it and takes a puff. She hands it over to* BERNADETTE *who takes a puff.* BERNADETTE *offers to* SEBASTIAN *who takes a puff. He chokes.*

Thought you had a better gag reflex.

SEBASTIAN: So did I.

BERNADETTE *starts singing John Denver's 'Take Me Home, Country Roads'.*

SEBASTIAN *and* MARIE *join in, substituting West Australia in place of West Virginia in the lyrics.*

The siblings smile as they sing. It's the first time they feel connected.

MARIE: Nan would be rolling around in her grave if she knew what we were doing.

SEBASTIAN: Well I'm going to hell anyway. Might as well join the rest of the alcoholics of this family.

MARIE: Once I caught her drunk.

BERNADETTE: What? When?

MARIE: Right after Mum went to hospital the second time. I think she had an argument with Pop or Aunt Mildred. But I came home early from school because I faked having my period to get out of swim class, and she was here at the table and had downed a bottle of Cinzano.

SEBASTIAN: [*correctly pronouncing*] Cinzano darl, Cinzano.

MARIE: I had to carry her to bed. She swore me to secrecy and said if I told you guys, she would report me to Jesus.

SEBASTIAN: As if that would've stopped you.

MARIE: She also gave me fifty dollars from Pop's horse winnings.

BERNADETTE: I caught her and Pop having a moonyin.

MARIE: Ew!

SEBASTIAN: Gross!

How?

BERNADETTE: I came home late from school and accidentally let in the cat, and I couldn't get it out. SO I walked into Nan's room to ask her and there was her and Pop … having a moonyin.

MARIE: It's bad enough we have to hear about Mum's antics. But Nan?

BERNADETTE: It was actually a relief to know there was passion. She was always threatening to leave Pop.

SEBASTIAN: I think Nan knew I was gay. I mean, it would probably be impossible not to suspect after she caught me with a cucumber and a picture of white Jesus.

MARIE: That's a one-way ticket to hell.

BERNADETTE: What did Nan do?

SEBASTIAN: She did this …

SEBASTIAN *tsk-sighs.*

And we never spoke about it again. That's when I started to pretend I was into Mary-Ann to save face.

BERNADETTE *tsk-sighs.*

MARIE *tsk-sighs.*

They all start to laugh. Drugs probably taking effect.

BERNADETTE: You all need therapy.

MARIE: You broke the pact, Bernadette.

BERNADETTE: To hell with the pact. I took all the emergency phone calls from Mum.

SEBASTIAN: Even in daylight savings?

BERNADETTE: She don't believe in it.

BERNADETTE, SEBASTIAN *and* MARIE: [*together*] It fades the curtains!

SEBASTIAN: You know in Europe—

MARIE *and* BERNADETTE: [*together*] No!

MARIE: No more Europe stories.

SEBASTIAN: Shut ya traps, ya moles. In Europe, I went to a therapist.

MARIE: You too?

SEBASTIAN: Well she was more a psychic but I did tell my life story and she said I had no hope and told me to leave but was nice to get it out.

MARIE: I booked the kids into a child psychologist.

BERNADETTE: The twins aren't even one.

MARIE: I'm scared they'll be traumatised by me. I can't have that. My mother-in-law is very judgey.

BERNADETTE: So we're all fucked.

MARIE: I'm not.

SEBASTIAN: You kind of are.

Beat.

But that just makes you family, Marie.

MARIE: What are we going to do with Mum.

BERNADETTE: Sing, dance, live in denial. When in Rome.

They start to sing 'Take Me Home, Country Roads' again. And again, they insert West Australia in the lyrics.

IZZY walks in. It's another side of the family he hasn't seen. He's warmed by it. He desperately wants to join in and he does so, inserting Western Sydney into the lyrics.

Everyone looks at IZZY.

IZZY: God I feel like a rum and coke.

The song finishes. Back to reality.

SEBASTIAN: I miss Nan.

BERNADETTE *offers* IZZY *a puff of the joint.*

IZZY: Oh no thanks. Doesn't agree with me.

BERNADETTE: You've never tried it so how would you know?

IZZY: I really took to those talking giraffe drug education videos in school. One joint would probably send me in a spiral, become homeless, sleep in a park, get thrown into jail. And where does it end? Ice? Crack? Prosecco?

SEBASTIAN: You really took to that giraffe.

BERNADETTE: If you're looking for a more wholesome time you can always go join Dawn and Mildred in the caravan.

MARIE: Oh that stupid caravan.

SEBASTIAN: No, no … the caravan of Adelaide dreams.

BERNADETTE: Wait till I tell her I've listed it on buy and sell.

MARIE: Another tantrum awaits.

IZZY: I'd buy it if I could.

SEBASTIAN: For what purpose?

IZZY: Something romantic about driving the endless road, camping under the stars. Showering in waterholes, coming across those standalone service stations, going in for beer, everyone staring at you because you're not local but you give them a nod and they nod back and you drive on, sweat on your forehead and flies on your back.

BERNADETTE, SEBASTIAN *and* MARIE *laugh.*

SEBASTIAN: That does not sound romantic at all. That's shit! That's *so* shit!

MARIE: [*to* IZZY] The big city boy wants to go bush?

BERNADETTE: Yet you became an accountant.

IZZY: Dad thought it would be a good career choice.

BERNADETTE *takes a swig.*

BERNADETTE: One day Izzy you'll make a decision for yourself. Dream for yourself.

IZZY *is hurt.*

IZZY: I can dream for myself.

SEBASTIAN *digs through the box. He pulls something out.*

SEBASTIAN: Speaking of dreams … Marie's yearbook!

MARIE: That's the rubbish pile Sebastian.

SEBASTIAN: Ahhh. Marie Osborn. Achievements: Belle of the Ball. We're calling beauty contests achievements?

MARIE: Beautiful people make the world visually better.

SEBASTIAN: Future goals. Let me guess … farmer's wife. President of Geraldton Mums and Bubs Facebook page. Pamphlet hander-outerer for John Trudgett? And the answer is: [*reading*] to travel the world. [*Realising*] Well you got as far as … Perth?

MARIE *snatches the book.*

MARIE: Stop.

SEBASTIAN: You could have come visit me in Portugal.

MARIE: For what? For you to criticise me in person. I wasn't a talented musician or smart enough for university so the joke's on me right. You got to live out your dream and see the world, I married a financially secure farmer.

IZZY: Nothing wrong with playing it safe.

BERNADETTE *laughs.*

BERNADETTE: Izzy, go back to Western Sydney. It's safe for you there.

IZZY: Why? Is this about your mum and I kissing? I didn't want that.

BERNADETTE: [*laughing*] I don't care about my mother kissing my fiancé. Ex-fiancé … She just did that to get back at me for controlling her. That's who she is. She used you and you willingly went with it even though I told you not to be alone in the same room.

IZZY: Fine. I know now.

BERNADETTE: It doesn't matter.

IZZY: Why?

BERNADETTE: Because I can't love you.

> IZZY *is stunned.*

> DAWN *comes marching in.*

DAWN: Alright. Let's have it out. You and me Bernadette. Let's binyardi [fight].

BERNADETTE: What, you want us to fight on the street?

> DAWN *takes off her shoes and earrings.*

I'm trying to hold your life together.

DAWN: Then why are there queer people looking at my van?

SEBASTIAN: Queer gay or queer strange?

DAWN: Mung-beans!

BERNADETTE: They're buyers.

DAWN: You're not selling my van. That's my dream.

MARIE: Here we go.

SEBASTIAN: It was their idea! I had a dream of driving you in that van to Mardi Gras.

IZZY: Why can't you just let her have the van? She wants the van.

DAWN: That's right. Thank you Izzy.

BERNADETTE: Are you both right? I'm too smashed for this.

DAWN: Smashed?

BERNADETTE: Yes I'm smashed! I'm having a moment of enjoyment in this bleak fucking town.

DAWN: And yet you judge me.

BERNADETTE: Dawn. You were never going to hit the road. You know this. I know this. Marie and Sebastian know this. Even Aunt Mildred, bless her drunk racist soul, knows this. You were going to end up just outside of town and have a breakdown because it's all overwhelming, and you'll marry some guy on the side of the road because of your toxic co-dependency and then he'll get sick of you and your hot and cold moods and dump you and you cry and call for help, you'll come home, crawl into bed and stay there for three months. But this time Nan's not here to pick up the pieces and clean up the mess. She's dead and I don't have half her patience.

MARIE: Wow.

SEBASTIAN: Geez.

IZZY: Bernadette.

BERNADETTE: Don't make me out to be the arsehole of the family. I'm keeping this family together.

MARIE: Language.

DAWN: You've been nasty and harsh … but you've never been cruel, Bernadette.

MILDRED *walks in.*

MILDRED: Seems those ordinary looking people weren't interested in your van or my ibis story.

BERNADETTE: There, your van stays. Not so cruel after all.

DAWN: For how long! You might as well put a rope around my neck because you've all killed me. Except you Izzy.

IZZY: Thanks.

DAWN: Sebastian!

SEBASTIAN: You're talking to me now?

DAWN: Put my funeral song on!

DAWN *rummages through the box of magazines and pulls out a replica of Diana's wedding dress and puts it on.*

BERNADETTE: We're not having your funeral.

DAWN: [*defiantly*] CD two, track three. Marie, get the flowers. Clear the table.

MARIE: If I do, will you allow me to never come back here?

DAWN: Yes.

IZZY: Maybe I should leave.

SEBASTIAN: You're in this with us. Sinking ship buddies.

DAWN: Aunt Mildred. Continue drinking your whiskey.

MILDRED: I plan too. What are we doing?

DAWN: We're acting out my funeral.

MILDRED: Lucky I'm still in my mourning clothes.

> MILDRED *takes a seat.*

DAWN: Sebastian zip me up. Marie—veil!

MARIE: Just like Princess Di Mum.

DAWN: Izzy! You're doing my eulogy! Bernadette has proven she is inhuman—

> *Mildred's phone rings*

IZZY: I don't think I should …

MILDRED: [*into the phone*] Vern, Dawnie's having her funeral.

SEBASTIAN: Song is ready.

DAWN: Press play.

BERNADETTE: [*to* DAWN] Don't do it. Don't you lay down.

> SEBASTIAN *and* MARIE *follow* DAWN*'s funeral march.* DAWN *lies down on the ground. Arms in rest in peace.*

Get up. Get up now.

IZZY: She's in the RIP position, it would be a shame to mess with that commitment. Give her something.

MARIE: Just let her do it. It will help.

BERNADETTE: This is not normal.

MARIE: It's normal for us.

BERNADETTE: You're enabling her.

MILDRED: Vern says hi, Dawnie and good luck on the funeral.

DAWN: Thanks Uncle Vern, all the best with your back.

MILDRED: [*into the phone*] Did you hear that?

DAWN: Sebastian, turn it up.

BERNADETTE: Don't do it, Sebastian.

MILDRED: [*into the phone*] She said all the best with your back!

SEBASTIAN: I'm sorry Dettie. I need her acceptance. It's the Catholic guilt in gay old me.

MILDRED: [*into the phone*] Not your bike, why would she be interested in your bike when she's topping herself, for God's sake.

MARIE: This phone call will never end.

MILDRED: [*into the phone*] I'll call you back.

DAWN: Marie.

Sacha Horler and Valerie Bader in Belvoir's production of Cursed! *(Photo by Luke Currie-Richardson)*

BERNADETTE: Marie?

MARIE: I actually feel sorry for her.

DAWN: Marie. Flowers.

> MARIE, *without enthusiasm, chucks flowers onto* DAWN.

Izzy. Eulogy.

BERNADETTE: [*to* IZZY] You're not a part of this.

> BERNADETTE *eyes* IZZY. *Will he do it?*

IZZY: I am a part of this. And I do have a backbone.

> *He clears his throat.*

Although I'm just an ex, Dawn really welcomed me into the family. She even sung to me with a dildo. And kissed me in the caravan. A little tongue.

MILDRED: I'm gonna need a top up.

IZZY: She gave clothes 'cause I came here with none. She cared so much she ironed my board shorts. I've never seen anyone iron board shorts before. She made sure I was comfortable. Washed my sheets every morning. Vacuumed my room. Even when I was still asleep. She just wanted things clean for me. And that's really nice. I've not had a family like that, not one that talks so openly as you. Best I get out of my dad is the rugby score. I appreciate you, Dawn.

> DAWN *is overcome with emotion. She stands up.*

DAWN: That's the nicest thing anyone has ever said to me.

SEBASTIAN: Really?

> *And ... in a split decision ...* DAWN *kisses* IZZY. *Again.*

MARIE: Whoa!

SEBASTIAN: Shit!

> IZZY *jumps back.*

> *Everyone turns to* BERNADETTE *waiting for her reaction. She gets up and walks out.*

> *Blackout.*

SCENE FOUR—PERISHING IN THE SEA

The southerly winds pick up. A dark storm is on the horizon.

MARIE *sets the table.* SEBASTIAN *makes a call.*

SEBASTIAN: Still no answer. I think she's abandoned us. She didn't even come to see Izzy off. He'll never come back to Geraldton. He fit in so well in his Bintang singlet.

MARIE: I hope Bernadette is dead.

SEBASTIAN: You don't mean that.

MARIE: Bernadette's abandoned us. So much for therapy, all she's done is call me selfish. I'm a mother. I'm the most selfless person here.

SEBASTIAN: You know she called me all those things too.

MARIE: Yeah but we're talking about me here. And now Izzy has left. Aunt Mildred doesn't look like she's leaving. And Mum is out of control. Bernadette ruined everything.

SEBASTIAN: She'll come back.

MARIE: Sebastian stop living oblivious to everything! She's not coming back. She's left you and me to look after Mum.

SEBASTIAN: I can't move back here. I've got ... opera singing.

MARIE: Yeah right. I'm just saying, throw your passport away because there's no way I'm doing this by myself.

SEBASTIAN: Shit.

MARIE: Bernadette better be dead. Don't think I'm going to her funeral either. I'll go to the morgue. I'll go look at her body and I'll say … [*whispering*] 'Bernadette, you're a c-word.'

SEBASTIAN: If you're gonna say it, at least say it with a bit of oomph. Embrace your inner Gero.

MARIE: Bernadette. You're a … You're a …

But MARIE *can't.*

You're being really inconvenient.

SEBASTIAN: You've got her there.

MARIE: Well I'm not like you or this town or this family and maybe I like it that way.

SEBASTIAN: Don't you get tired? Spending all that energy running away.

MARIE: Pot, kettle, gay Sebastian.

SEBASTIAN: That was for religious persecution reasons. You just want to tear down this house because you don't want to be reminded that you are part of us. Even in high school I remember you telling your mole friends, including Celia with the flat forehead, that we weren't your family and you were adopted.

MARIE: Well it's not like this family wanted me. I came back every second weekend to check on Nan. I cooked Nan dinner Saturday night. Roast chicken with vegetables. And still you were the favourite. And still Bernadette was the carer. Maybe I didn't want to acknowledge this family because you all don't acknowledge me. You haven't even asked once about your nieces. You haven't even come to meet them. At least Mum came for two days, Bernadette came for a week but I needed you to reassure me, to reassure them. Because what else have I got to pass down to them but a curse?

MARIE *shows* SEBASTIAN *a photo.*

SEBASTIAN: Is that them?

MARIE: Yes.

SEBASTIAN *is overwhelmed.*

SEBASTIAN: They are quite good looking.

MARIE: Of course. They're bi-racial.

SEBASTIAN: Which one is which?

MARIE: On the left is Mila and on the right is Lahni.

SEBASTIAN: Lahni has my freckle.

SEBASTIAN points to his freckle on his cheek.

MARIE: She does too. And she's a little B-I-T-C-H so personality fits.

SEBASTIAN: I'm an Uncle … wait, I'm more than that. I'm a Guncle.

MARIE starts getting teary.

SEBASTIAN wants to hug her. He touches her shoulder.

MILDRED and DAWN come in with a casserole of apricot chicken.

MILDRED: Well he went on and on and I said to him, I said love if you're gonna get your prostate tested, do it with a real doctor this time. What was it you asked again?

DAWN: I asked if you wanted some apricot chicken.

MILDRED: Right—oh yes please.

Everyone sits.

DAWN: Let us pray.

Everyone bows their head.

Dear Lord and Nan, thank you for this meal of apricot chicken kindly given to us by Carol from number ten. I pray for the poor kids especially the ones addicted to ice. I pray for Sebastian for gracing the stages of Paris with his opera singing. I pray for Marie and my grandchildren, may they be doctors or mechanics one day. I pray for Aunt Mildred who is in deep mourning for her sister and Uncle Vern for his back. I pray for Izzy, who has been run out of town, the greatest son-in-law I'll never have. And Lord, I pray for my daughter Bernadette who has abandoned us in our time of need. Nan, you ought to know that she's a mole. Amen. Shall we eat?

Isn't this wonderful? Family time. Real family time. Isn't that right, Aunt Mildred.

DAWN starts serving the plates.

MILDRED: I suppose.

DAWN reaches the last, extra plate; Bernadette's plate. She stops. Bernadette's absence is felt.

DAWN: Hey …

SEBASTIAN: I forgot, Bernadette wasn't here.

> DAWN *ignores the extra plate. She continues serving. She takes a seat.*

It's not like her to be gone for this long. She usually gets over it.

DAWN: She's probably back in Sydney, telling everyone there that I stole her man and I stole her land. Forget her! Aunt Mildred, you were telling me about the family tree?

MILDRED: Oh yes. Our great-great-great uncle was a baker. Came over in the gold rush. He offed himself with a gun but the family said it was a baking accident. Then our grandmother was always leg up on the lounge with nerves, Poor Granny Mary. Good cook though—made great scones. Rumour is she offed herself in the oven. We even have a backyard abortionist a few lines back, she was sent to the loony bin but I don't think there was anything wrong with her. But she offed herself. Stabbed herself ten times.

DAWN: Ten times?

> *No-one knows what to say.*

SEBASTIAN: What if Bernadette's hung herself?

DAWN: Too windy. You can't hang yourself when the southerly's in, I've tried.

> *Everyone eats in silence. Worry grows. Bite by bite anxiety grows.*

> DAWN *pushes her plate forward.*

It's bloody dry. Bloody Carol. I'll tell her. I'll march down to number ten and say Carol … I'll say Carol. I wouldn't feed this to my dogs. I mean, how hard is it to make apricot BLOODY CHICKEN!

MARIE: She's used the wrong tinned apricots.

DAWN: Too right, Marie. Everyone knows you use the top shelf apricots. It's not bloody hard.

SEBASTIAN: Thought it tasted dry. *Cough. Cough.*

MILDRED: Tastes quite nice to me.

DAWN: Sebastian go find your sister.

SEBASTIAN: I thought you didn't want her to come back?

DAWN: She needs to hear about Carol's apricot chicken.

SEBASTIAN: I don't think she'll care.

MARIE *stands up.*

MARIE: Well she'll want to care. She'll wanna care that Carol ruined the apricot chicken. Carol's ruined everything.

DAWN: Yes! Everything!

SEBASTIAN *gets up.*

SEBASTIAN: I'm gonna find her.

MARIE: Carol?

SEBASTIAN: Fuck Carol!

DAWN: Yes, fuck Carol.

SEBASTIAN: No, I'm gonna find Bernadette. I'm gonna tell her about Carol's apricot chicken. How it's as dry as Carol's moot. Because fuck Carol and her dry old moot. If we're gonna sink, then we're going down together. Marie. You're on the ship too.

MARIE: I'm on the ship?

DAWN: You were always on the bloody ship, Marie!

MARIE: I'm on this ship too! FUCK CAROL.

SEBASTIAN *and* MARIE *march out. There's silence for a moment.* DAWN *takes a bite of her dinner.*

MILDRED: Who the devil is Carol?

DAWN: Nobody.

MILDRED: Oh please, Dawn. I may be drunk but I'm not stupid.

DAWN: Look what I've got.

DAWN *pulls out a passion pop bottle from behind the piano.*

Da da da! Those bloody kids drive me crazy.

MILDRED: My Douglas hasn't spoken to me since I refused to put up the bail.

DAWN: Cousin Dougie is in jail? I thought he was in Thailand opening up a school for the poor?

MILDRED: I just tell people that. No, he's in the clink, back on the ice. Policemen knocking on our door asking for him. They found him lying in some swampland, south of the river. God knows what he was doing down there. He asked us to bail him out and I said like hell. I'm not going all the way down south of the river. I blame his father. Vern always over indulged in him. That's why he could never settle down with a girl.

DAWN: I would have settled down with Ken, you know. We could have had a happy life.

MILDRED: Which one was he?

DAWN: The Chinese farmer. He was from a hard-working family. Came here with nothing when he was ten and his family set up a tomato farm. We had a whirlwind romance, like Charles and Di in the early years. He was desperado to fit in and be an Aussie so he joined a pub band as a drummer and rode a motorbike. I was having a night out at the disco. We were having a bloody ball—singing and dancing. It was that song 'Am I Ever Gonna See Your Face Again' ... and you know us in the crowd yells back 'no way, get fucked, fuck off!' Across the room I made eyes for Ken, banging away on the drums. It wasn't long till I was taking rides on the back of his motorbike. We rode around the lighthouse, rolled around in the sand dunes and listened to rock and roll. Incidentally I got knocked up with Marie on the back of his motorbike to the second half of Meatloaf's 'I Would Do Anything For Love'. No wonder she came out bitter. We got married fast, shotgun wedding. His family, the traditional ones, came to visit and just as I was serving them up my famous sausage casserole, they told Ken, in front of me, that he could do better. It was all downhill from there. It wasn't long before Ken quit the band, cut his hair and left. My mother just did the—

DAWN *tsk-sighs.*

Another divorce. Nan with her Catholic judgement and her I told you so's. Broken hearts and empty record players. There was no appreciating the good after that. Not even Helen Reddy could pull me out of that hole.

MILDRED: I'll let you in on a secret Dawn.

DAWN: What?

MILDRED: As you get older you realise that it all doesn't matter. You know, this year I've been to fourteen funerals. The more you go to them the more you start to wonder ... if all your friends are dead—who's going to come to your funeral? I always thought at least Val will be there. We've had our disagreements, sister stuff but she'd always come to my funeral and mourn me. Now I'm the one mourning her. With Dougie in the clink and Vern and his never-ending back problems, he'll go before me, you and your kids are the only family I have.

DAWN: They'll be thrilled to hear that.

MILDRED: In the end we're all worm food. That's as simple as it gets. From Hitler to the Pope. From your mother to … that one-eyed cat you had in the eighties.

DAWN: Doris Day. Poor Doris. Hung herself in the venetian blinds. Even our pets are fucked. Ha!

MILDRED: I guess there's no hope for any of us.

DAWN: I can pinpoint the day Bernadette changed. She rang me one day when I was in the nuthouse in absolute hysterics. Going on about the bloody Batavia.

MILDRED: The ship?

DAWN: Yes she was obsessed with it. Always had her head in the book reading about the shipwreck and the mutiny. And look I don't condone murder, but being stuck on an island on the edge of earth with the Dutch, I understand the reasons.

MILDRED: Too right. No sense of humour, the Dutch.

DAWN: I think it's their accent.

>   DAWN *badly imitates the accent.*

MILDRED: Right.

DAWN: Bernadette had this big talk in school and she prepared for weeks. And then the day comes, and my mother, her nan, tells her she can't come. And I couldn't come, I was locked up. Sebastian and Marie were off doing their own thing. That's when she rang me crying, in pure panic. The first thing she said 'I hate you and I hate this family.' And I said … I said … 'Good'.

>   DAWN *starts tearing up.*

I gave my kids resilience, schooled them in hard knocks. And if Bernadette has offed herself, I'll be really disappointed because I taught her to survive this monstrous world and isn't that the most wonderful lesson, better than love.

>   DAWN *turns up the music. 'Angel from Montgomery' by Bonnie Raitt plays.*

>   BERNADETTE *walks in. Soaking wet.* DAWN *looks her up and down. She turns off the music.*

You try and Virginia Woolf yourself?

BERNADETTE: Aunt Mildred, could you give my mother and I a moment?

MILDRED: I need a smoke anyway.

DAWN: Didn't know you smoke?

MILDRED: Only after whiskey and sex.

> MILDRED *exits.*

DAWN: If you've come to tell me I'm a bad mother, I already know it.

BERNADETTE: Good. I'm a bad daughter. I'm a bad granddaughter. I'm a bad sister. I'm a bad fiancé and an even worse ex-fiancé. I went to the ocean and waded in, I cursed your names into the waves and screamed into the wind and I went under.

DAWN: No rocks?

BERNADETTE: No rocks.

> DAWN *is overcome with relief; she tries to hide her tears.*

Are you crying?

DAWN: No, it's the wind. Plays on my hayfever.

BERNADETTE: I dove in, let the current take me and it spat me back to shore where I opened my eyes and saw … the fucking lighthouse. And I realised something. I don't have a funeral song. But I know your funeral songs. I know Sebastian's, I know Marie's. And so I'm lying underneath the lighthouse thinking of a funeral song when it occurs to me how fucking mad this all is … And how much I miss my family because they're the only ones I know that would understand how important, yet crazy, it is to have a funeral song. Mum, you've survived everything that's thrown at you. You survived three husbands, three divorces, a few trips to the mental hospital, false accusation at the canteen …

DAWN: Carol's apricot chicken.

BERNADETTE: So maybe in this house of madness, the mad truth is that crude humour, no rules, kissing ex-fiancé, fake funerals …

DAWN: I'm really sorry about that,

BERNADETTE: Maybe all that madness might have actually saved us.

DAWN: God help us.

BERNADETTE: I've lost everything. I can't lose you.

> DAWN *is full of pride.*

DAWN: You're not a bad daughter.

BERNADETTE: Oh please. I'm a shit daughter.

DAWN: A little bit.

BERNADETTE: Get out of this place, sail away, go across the Nullarbor, go to Adelaide, go get married, take your damn meds, you're a grown adult, just go and survive.

DAWN: What if I can't?

BERNADETTE: We come back here, start again and joke about it in three years' time. Remember that time Dawn tried to cross the Nullarbor and she married some backpacker.

DAWN: I bet he's called Britt.

BERNADETTE: Britt the Kiwi backpacker.

DAWN: You see that. You get your sense of humour from me.

BERNADETTE: Thank fuck. The world would be depressing otherwise.

> BERNADETTE *realises something.*

Oh shit.

DAWN: What?

BERNADETTE: I just realised my funeral song.

DAWN: What is it?

BERNADETTE: Fucking 'Fur Elise'.

DAWN: Oh Beethoven can get fucked.

> DAWN *hugs* BERNADETTE.

> MILDRED *walks in with* SEBASTIAN.

MILDRED: And that's how Great Uncle Mal got done for being a pedo …

SEBASTIAN: Fascinating. Please never tell that story to me again.

> SEBASTIAN *sees that* BERNADETTE *is soaking wet.*

DAWN: She didn't Virginia Woolf herself!

> SEBASTIAN *runs to them and hugs them.*

SEBASTIAN: I'm sorry. All I could think about was this Catholic guilt of not telling you and Mum.

BERNADETTE: Not telling us what?

SEBASTIAN: I lied. I'm not really an opera star. I quit opera school. I have anxiety. I can't please you. I don't want to disappoint you but … but … I'm a flight attendant.

> DAWN *considers it.*

DAWN: Oh Sebastian. You could never disappoint me. You're my favourite.

They hug.

MARIE *walks in and sees* SEBASTIAN, BERNADETTE *and* DAWN *hugging.*

MARIE: This is mutiny! You're kicking me out, aren't you?

Everyone turns to MARIE.

BERNADETTE: No it's not what—

MARIE: Bernadette, this is your fault. You coming back. You being the captain. You pushing me out. Well I am this family. And I am this town. And I can binyadi. And you're nothing but a *black cunt.*

SEBASTIAN: Good oomph.

MARIE *launches at* BERNADETTE. BERNADETTE *fights back.* SEBASTIAN *jumps in. They fight as siblings do—pulling and pinching.*

DAWN *pours another glass for* MILDRED.

As the siblings fight they edge close to the ashes. BERNADETTE *is pushed and falls into the piano. Nan's ashes scatter on the ground.*

Everyone is shocked.

MARIE: Is that Nan?

MARIE *gets up.*

Beat.

DAWN *gets up. We think she's going to scream. But she gets the dust-buster and starts vacuuming.*

She empties the ashes back into the box.

DAWN: Aunt Mildred? Would you like a ham sandwich and a cup of tea?

Everything is back to normal.

SCENE FIVE—NEW HORIZONS

The lounge room is sparse. Everything is gone except for the piano. BERNADETTE, MARIE *and* DAWN *sit around a camping table and chairs.* SEBASTIAN *stands before them dressed in the silk kimono.*

DAWN: Do it Sebastian, I want you to perform for your life.

SEBASTIAN: Do I have to?

DAWN: Yes, the only way you'll overcome this stage anxiety is if you practice. I've already told Marg at the canteen how good you are at it. Now show me.

    SEBASTIAN *nods.*

SEBASTIAN: Fine.

DAWN: He's going to show us!

    SEBASTIAN *gets in the zone like any performer.*

SEBASTIAN: Red leather, yellow leather. Unique New York. Okay ready.

    SEBASTIAN *clears his throat. As he speaks he performs the accompanying actions.*

Your safety is important to us. Please secure your seatbelt, click together like this. In the unlikely event of an emergency, oxygen masks will fall. Secure over your head like this. This aircraft has three emergency exits, one at the front, one in the middle, and one at the end. Follow the floor lighting to your closest exit. Life jackets can be found under your seat. Pull the tabs to inflate and for further inflation, blow like this.

DAWN: I bet you blow like that.

SEBASTIAN: A light and a whistle are attached to attract attention. Please make sure your bag is stowed and your tray table secured. [*As himself*] And then I serve the cunts tea and biscuits.

    Everyone claps and cheers. SEBASTIAN *bows and takes in the applause.*

MARIE: Lovely.

SEBASTIAN: Thank you very much.

    Everyone claps.

MARIE: Do we get family discount on flights?

SEBASTIAN: Yes. All you can fly is economy. [*To* MARIE] Are we going or what?

MARIE: Yeah, yeah hang on.

DAWN: Where are you two going?

MARIE: The twins await and I miss them.

DAWN: And you?

SEBASTIAN: I have discovered there's a whole new way of picking up …
being the gay uncle. It will get me lots of cock.

DAWN: Music to a mother's ears! But don't forget Mardi Gras. I'm going
on the parents and allies float. I have this really nice red thong …

SEBASTIAN: Yeah Mum, apart from just confirming my homosexuality,
I really don't need to know the details.

DAWN: I'll see yas at Easter …

MARIE: [*looking around*] You know I will miss this house. Lost my
virginity there.

> *She points to where* SEBASTIAN *is standing.*

DAWN: Like mother, like daughter.

SEBASTIAN: And brother.

MARIE: I'm out.

> SEBASTIAN *and* MARIE *argue on their way out.*

SEBASTIAN: [*excitedly*] I shotgun music.

MARIE: [*offstage*] Hell no. I'm the driver.

SEBASTIAN: Shut up Marie.

> MARIE *and* SEBASTIAN *leave. There's quiet in the house.*

DAWN: I think you should do me your Batavia speech. To me and Nan.

> DAWN *drags the ashes over, they wait as an audience.* BERNADETTE
> *thinks.*

BERNADETTE: I'm so sick of the Batavia. It's actually really morbid. It's
just white people massacring each other for gold and power.

DAWN: Sounds about right.

BERNADETTE: Piano movers are coming tomorrow and that will be the
last of it. You don't want to spend the last night in Nan's house?

> DAWN *picks up the ashes and moves to the door.*

DAWN: God no. I hated this place. It isn't special to me. Knock it down
and start anew. I got plans. Everything I need is in my van. Oh I forgot.

> DAWN *pulls out a dildo from a box.*

> DAWN *gets to the door.*

I've got me. I've got Patrick. I've got Nan. Adelaide … here I roar.

> DAWN *exits with the dildo and Nan's ashes.*

Quiet.

BERNADETTE *feels the space.*

She sits at the piano. She feels the memories as she feels the keys beneath her fingers.

She plays the first bit of 'Fur Elise'. She still has it!

BERNADETTE *looks up and sees* IZZY *standing there.*

BERNADETTE: Izzy … you're back.

IZZY *pulls out a letter with multiple pages, clears his throat and starts to read.*

IZZY: I went back to Sydney. I went straight to my family, my sister was having her kid's birthday and they started talking about renovating the back room for a play room. Dad said it would add value to the land. Then my sister told me I should invest. And they started talking about plans and off the plan. And I realised something … My family is really boring. Did you know about the first home buyers fund for example?

BERNADETTE: Funnily enough, the thought of mortgages makes me depressed.

IZZY *looks up to* BERNADETTE *and realises he's losing her attention. He skips a few pages.*

IZZY: Then I'll skip this. This bit really isn't important … life in Sydney, life as an accountant, life in general, life meaning, stock prices, blackfella curses, Dawn's theories on Diana and Charles.

IZZY *drops his cards. He doesn't need them. He speaks from the heart.*

And then I crashed here, there was death, two funerals, an outing, inappropriate kisses.

IZZY *smiles. He turns around, readying his performance.*

But I love you and this family. And to prove to you I do …

He starts his performance. He takes out a speaker and plays 'Delta Dawn' on his phone.

IZZY *starts lip-syncing, using a lighthouse ornament as a microphone. Sexy dancing.*

BERNADETTE *laughs. They take each other's hands and exit into their room.*

NAN *comes out and stands, feeling the music. She smiles. The curse is broken.*

And the lighthouse light continues to cycle. On and on and on.

Fade to black.

THE END

www.currency.com.au

Visit Currency Press' website now to:

- Buy your books online
- Browse through our full list of titles, from plays to screenplays, books on theatre, film and music, and more
- Choose a play for your school or amateur performance group by cast size and gender
- Obtain information about performance rights
- Find out about theatre productions and other performing arts news across Australia
- For students, read our study guides
- For teachers, access syllabus and other relevant information
- Sign up for our email newsletter

The performing arts publisher

www.ingramcontent.com/pod-product-compliance
Lightning Source LLC
Chambersburg PA
CBHW050019090426
42734CB00021B/3330